English Education and the Radicals
1780–1850

STUDENTS LIBRARY OF EDUCATION

English Education and the Radicals 1780-1850

Harold Silver

Professor of Education (Social History),
Chelsea College, University of London

ROUTLEDGE & KEGAN PAUL
LONDON AND BOSTON

First published in 1975
by Routledge & Kegan Paul Ltd
Broadway House, 68-74 Carter Lane,
London EC4V 5EL and
9 Park Street,
Boston, Mass. 02108, USA
Set in Linotype Pilgrim
and printed in Great Britain by
Northumberland Press Limited, Gateshead
© Harold Silver 1975

ISBN 0 7100 8212 6

THE STUDENTS LIBRARY OF EDUCATION has been designed to meet the needs of students of Education at Colleges of Education and at University Institutes and Departments. It will also be valuable for practising teachers and educationists. The series takes full account of the latest developments in teacher-training and of new methods and approaches in education. Separate volumes will provide authoritative and up-to-date accounts of the topics within the major fields of sociology, philosophy and history of education, educational psychology, and method. Care has been taken that specialist topics are treated lucidly and usefully for the non-specialist reader. Altogether, the Students Library of Education will provide a comprehensive introduction and guide to anyone concerned with the study of education, and with educational theory and practice.

Education does not only go on in schools, colleges and universities; social, political and religious movements in the wider society may often have a profound educative effect—shaping new outlooks, patterns of living, human aspirations. This is certainly true of the period Harold Silver covers in this book. Economic and technological change in the early nineteenth century profoundly affected social relationships, disrupting traditional forms of pre-industrial society, and bringing into being new social classes whose interests sometimes appeared to coincide, more often to stand in opposition to each other. Education now began to be seen as a weapon through which specific class interests might be realised. In this period the relation between education and politics was, perhaps, closer and more explicit than at any other period in our history.

In this volume, Professor Silver interprets these developments, clarifying the complex relationships, changing over time, between different social classes and their educational theories and initiatives. It is, in some respects, a dramatic story, reflecting the harsh conditions which gave rise to Peterloo, the earlier Owenite movement and culminating in Chartism. Such a study casts light on the crucial question of the relations between education and society.

It is to an understanding of this complex issue, as well as of the background to educational changes in the mid to late nineteenth century, that this book makes an original contribution.

BRIAN SIMON

Contents

Note

Attempts are often made to distinguish between radicalism as a general term and Radicalism as a specific nineteenth-century political movement. Radicalism is, however, too complex a phenomenon for differentiation by capital letter to have much meaning, and all distinctions are therefore indicated in this book by the use of an adjective where necessary—for example, political radicalism, working-class radicalism, Benthamite radicalism.

The references given in brackets in the text indicate the date of first publication of sources. Page references are sometimes those of a later edition—in which case the date of such editions is given in the bibliography.

Acknowledgments

I am indebted to Phillip McCann for helping to clarify some problems relating to the early part of this book; to Brian Simon for his comments on the draft—as well as for helping to coax the book into existence; to Rosemary Burbidge for help, among other things, with the pursuit of difficult detail; and to the librarians of the Centre for Science Education, Chelsea College, for their constant support—without which the task would have been immeasurably harder.

1

Root and branch reformers

A pioneer study of early radical politics traced the 'dawn of radicalism' in the period from the 1760s to the 1790s, the activities of Wilkes and Horne Tooke and Major Cartwright, the crusade for parliamentary reform and freedom of the press, Tom Paine, and support for the American Revolution of 1776 and the French Revolution of 1789. It described the early radicals as 'those who fought the good fight of Reform', to change a corrupt and ossified Parliament and constitution. The nineteenth-century radical reformer was—in the eyes of the defenders of the existing system—'a mixture of fiend, fanatic and felon, constantly plotting how he may overturn the institutions of society'. The radical, or 'root and branch reformer', was in reality, however, 'a politician who does effectually whatever he attempts, going to the root of the matter' (Daly, 1892, 1, 112-13). At the end of the eighteenth century the 'root of the matter' was seen as the need to reform Parliament, though political radicals always saw more or less clearly that other social improvements would flow from successful political reform. Through the reform of Parliament lay the extension of liberty and social justice, freedom from one or another form of social oppression or corruption. The radical, said G. J. Holyoake in the 1880s, was 'a man who has heroic unrest under injustice', even if he did not always have a coherent policy for ending oppression (Holyoake, 1881, 185). Radicalism, wrote one of the pioneers of modern British socialism, 'in its genuine sense of opposition to all class domination and a thorough organisation of the collective power of the people', had made great headway in the early nineteenth century (Hyndman, 1883, 206-7). The radicalism of the late eighteenth and early nineteenth centuries was, in fact, the harnessing of energies in protest against injustice and oppression, the pooling of effort to transform society.

Organisation for effective reform is neither uniquely British nor a product of the past two centuries. As a modern, continuous tradition, however, it can be identified clearly in Britain from the beginning of the 1780s. Out of a diffuse and unstable urban radicalism that had existed from the 1760s a new form of political organisation began to emerge:

> Horne Tooke and Major Cartwright may be said to have been the first who endeavoured to organize for practical purposes those who held Radical opinions. Major Cartwright ... in the year 1780 founded the Constitutional Society ... to give the public political information, and particularly to promote a recovery of what they conceived to be the lost rights of the people; meaning the right of representation in the House of Commons (Daly, 1892, 114).

The society for Constitutional Information, to give it its full title, followed the publication of Major Cartwright's *Take Your Choice!* in 1776, with its emphasis on political equality, on the need to eliminate political distinctions as 'causes for the elevation of some above the rest, prior to mutual agreement' (Cartwright, 1776, 3). Out of the search for effective organisation and clear objectives emerged not *a* radicalism, but *forms* of radicalism. Cartwright himself divided reformers into two camps, those who wanted modest reforms and those who wanted a thorough reform to permit 'a constitutional representation of the people in parliament', in other words the 'moderate reformists, and the constitutional reformists'. The moderates he also described as 'mock' or 'gradual' reformers; the constitutional reformers he also described as 'radical' reformers (Cartwright, 1812, 5, 21-2, 31). 'Radical', as an adjective to describe this type of reformer, had established itself in this way by the 1780s, though as a noun it was not to gain common currency for another forty or so years.

The distinction between radical and moderate reformers was intensified in the 1790s after the French Revolution and with the emergence of a distinctively popular radicalism in the first phase of the social changes accompanying the Industrial Revolution. From this point radical reform acquired a new content:

> The question posed in Great Britain up to 1789 was almost exclusively one of political rights ... and not of a change of social system. Not until we arrive at the second part of Tom Paine's *Rights of Man* do we find the first fundamental social programme put forward on behalf of the people since the days of Winstanley and the Diggers (Cole, 1953, 2-3).

Cartwright and his associates continued to assert that 'reform must be radical' (Union for Parliamentary Reform, 1812, 2), but during the Napoleonic wars new radical objectives began to be defined. To the left of the Whigs appeared the Benthamite (or 'utilitarian' or 'philosophic') radicals. From the 1790s, in the writings of Tom Paine,

3

William Godwin and others, had emerged an extensive tradition of articulate, far-reaching ideas of political and social reform, ideas which gained a new lease of life in the period after the war ended in 1815. It was in this period that the Tories coined the noun 'radical' as 'an offensive nickname for the revolutionary democrats' (Halévy, 1926, 68-9n). Radicalism had grown strong enough to be seen as a threat to the established order, to Church and State. In 1819 magistrates feared that the radicals were arming, that their aim was now 'not simply manhood suffrage and annual Parliaments; they sought, by this or by any other means, to restore the land to the community and abolish private property' (ibid., 67-8). James Mill, the leading Benthamite radical, in 1818 published a history of India, saturated—in his son's words—'with the opinions and modes of judgment of a democratic radicalism then regarded as extreme' (J. S. Mill, 1873, 21). An item in the Christian Socialist journal, Politics for the People, in 1848 objected to its being described by critics as 'very radical': 'the etymological definition of the word "Radical" is "that which is infixed as a root deeply." But ... this is not the sense which the objectors give to the word when they apply it to the Politics for the People.' Others, such as Chartists and radicals, might wish to uproot the national tree, but the Christian Socialists sought to bring people to 'consider the life that is in the old hidden root' (Politics for the People, no. 9, 1848, 158-9).

In the first half of the nineteenth century, therefore, the interpretation of radicalism, by its advocates and its enemies, assumed various forms. The radical could be seen as an agitator and a subversive, or as an upholder of popular and even ancient traditions, according to one's view of the social order, and of the desirability of preserving or altering it—and to what extent. From the later decades of the eighteenth century the pressures of social change brought programmes of radical reform increasingly to the centre of public debate. The definition of forms of radicalism came to be associated with the sharpening awareness of social class. The various traditions of radicalism were to be remoulded into the two key concepts of working-class and middle-class radicalism. Radicalism, social class and education became intertwined problems and concepts.

In the discussion of education during this period we are, of course, not merely concerned with schools. In addition to the various kinds of endowed and charity schools which existed in the late eighteenth century, as well as universities and academies, this period saw the emergence of new educational ideas and objectives, the educational impact of political organisations and publications, new forms of the dissemination of knowledge and of intellectual discussion and debate. It is an essential part of the argument, therefore, to see not only the existence or the emergence of educational institutions, but also the profound impact of new political and social forces, the appearance of new pressures for education in its broadest sense.

2

Radical reformers and education, 1780-1800

Early radical traditions

The reformers of the 1760s to the 1780s were for the most part concerned with an attack on an unrepresentative Parliament, with problems of taxation and the excessive power of the landed gentry. There was popular agitation, outstandingly in the campaign to reinstate John Wilkes in the House of Commons. There were political clubs and societies, pamphleteering and political organisation. Especially in the 1770s and 1780s the demands for parliamentary reform, both moderate and radical, grew more widespread and better organised. The reformers of this period 'helped to excite an interest and to set an example in popular organization for the purposes of securing constitutional reform. Even more important, perhaps, was the stimulus given to discussion in print' (Christie, 1962, 231). The objectives of the reformers were conceived in parliamentary and constitutional terms. For many of them the aim was what they saw as the restoration of ancient rights. For Major Cartwright, for example, the work of reform was the same as that which resulted in Magna Carta—'the reformists of this age are embarked in the identical work, and labouring to complete the identical task'. A return to 'solid Saxon simplicity', overthrown by the Norman conquest, was needed (Cartwright, 1812, 1). The appeal to ancient principle was to be a common theme in future radical movements. Thomas Attwood told a Scottish Chartist rally in 1838 that such meetings were 'part of the constitution of England.... They have existed from the earliest ages of our Saxon ancestors' (Wakefield, 1885, 327).

The change in the tenor of radical reform after 1789 must be seen in the context of traditions of democratic and radical ideals and action. Part of this tradition was that of the dissenters' struggle for social and political rights. Restrictions on the dissenters' right to preach and teach from the 1680s had led to the growth of an 'alternative' English educational system in the form of dissenting academies. Dissenting schoolmasters created academies which rivalled and surpassed the grammar schools in both curriculum and the quality of teaching. Excluded from Oxford and Cambridge, the children of dissenters found a more efficient and a more modern higher education both in the English academies and in the Scottish universities. Although the academies declined in the latter part of the eighteenth century, they represented a characteristic interest in education in the nonconformist communities. They had experimented with new curricula and teaching methods. Joseph Priestley, scientist and educationist, used his experience at Warrington Academy to contribute important views on modern educational practice to the literature of education. The essential curriculum for Priestley, unlike the endowed grammar schools, included not only Latin, but also mathematics, English, French, science, history and other subjects. His *Essay on a Course of Liberal Education* (1765) propounded just such a broad curriculum. In the rationalist tradition Priestley was concerned with

7

what he called 'the slowest of all processes—that of enlightening the minds of men' (Priestley, 1791, 439). The academies, in a tradition of liberal dissent, had aimed to train men in a spirit of moral and social responsibility.

The same tradition pervaded other intellectual and educational enterprises. It underlay the activities of the Birmingham men of science and industry who founded the Lunar Society in the mid-1760s as a focus of discussion of science, industry and related social issues. Similar groups, formal and informal, appeared elsewhere, bringing together mainly nonconformist industrialists, scientists and professional men. At Manchester, Dr Thomas Percival, a pioneer of health reform, began a discussion circle in the early 1770s which became the Manchester Literary and Philosophical Society in 1781. Men such as these had in many cases been educated at dissenting academies, and at Scottish or European universities. They sponsored educational developments. In Manchester, this included a College of Arts and Science in 1783 and an Academy in 1786. The dissenters supported and developed the Sunday school movement from 1780. By the late 1780s, therefore, the traditions of religious dissent and political radicalism had produced a range of institutions and activities in which ideas of social and political change circulated. The impact of the French Revolution was on a society in which long traditions of political, religious and social dissent were active, against a background of, and related to, important industrial and social changes.

The French Revolution and English radicalism

In its opening phase the French Revolution 'did not constitute a fresh principle of division in the confused party politics of England.... Many were pleased to bestow a patronising approval on an imitation, at the interval of a century, of the glorious English Revolution' (Brown, 1918, 37). But divisions soon appeared. The Rev. Richard Price, who had been a prominent supporter of the American Revolution, welcomed the French Revolution as a major event for human liberty. In November 1789 at a public meeting he moved a congratulatory address to the French National Assembly, welcoming the 'glorious example given in France to encourage other nations to assert the unalienable rights of mankind ... and to make the world free and happy' (Morgan, 1815, 155-6). The publication of Price's *Discourse* was to prove 'the first shot in an ideological battle that lasted for years' (Maccoby, 1955, 27), as the revolution took new directions, and anti-revolutionary opinion hardened in Britain.

The essential impact of the French Revolution was in bringing tangible objectives closer to hand for people already at odds with old tyrannies and new dimensions of social change, 'transferring from the order of things spiritual to the life here below the longing for justice and for happiness' (Cestre, 1906, 65). When Edmund Burke, in his *Reflections on the Revolution in France* in 1790 attacked Price, the revolution and its underlying principles, the response was a flood of ideas that profoundly changed the course of radical history. The flood contained, in fact was dominated by, Paine's *Rights of Man*, which Edward Thompson describes as 'one of the two foundation texts of the English working-class movement'—the other being Bunyan's *Pilgrim's Progress*. Bunyan and Paine, William Cobbett and Robert Owen, 'contributed most to the stock of ideas and attitudes which make up the raw material of the movement from 1790-1850' (Thompson, 1963, 31).

The *Rights of Man* was an appeal for reason and right government. The American and French Revolutions, said

9

Paine, 'have thrown a beam of light over the world'. Ignorance was being dispelled, and 'once dispelled, it is impossible to re-establish it ... though man may be *kept* ignorant, he cannot be *made* ignorant ... it has never yet been discovered how to make man *unknow* his knowledge, or *unthink* his thoughts'. Reason must prevail, Paine emphasised, above all in the affairs of government—including in the field of education:

> When, in countries that are called civilized, we see age going to the workhouse and youth to the gallows, something must be wrong in the system of government.... Civil government does not consist in executions; but in making such provision for the instruction of youth and the support of old age, as to exclude, as much as possible, profligacy from the one and despair from the other.

Under a well-regulated government, he concluded, a nation 'should permit none to remain uninstructed'. Only monarchical and aristocratic government 'requires ignorance for its support' (Paine, 1791, 86-7, 194, 224). Many other radical spokesmen resisted the notion of state intervention in education, but Paine had helped to inject into popular politics a commitment to social and educational advance based not only on political rights, but also on a set of social ideals. Ignorance had been identified as a prime enemy—a development of no small importance in a period when over a third of the population could not sign their names. The importance of Paine's contribution, however, lay in its impact on popular political organisation. The radical organisations of the 1790s distributed and discussed the *Rights of Man* and made its ideals of justice, reason and humanity common currency. Even if estimates of 200,000 copies of the *Rights of Man* in circulation by

1793, and of 1,500,000 copies of Part Two alone having been sold by Paine's death in 1809, are exaggerations, the circulation was large enough to give a whole new impetus to radical organisation, and it gave a new dimension to the anxiety of the authorities, who prosecuted it as seditious libel (Altick, 1957, 70-2).

Together with new ideas came new organisations. The old Constitutional Society took on a new lease of life. A Society of Friends of the People was created, mainly of Whigs, exclusive and with a high subscription. Other, more popular, reform organisations were set up in many towns—including Sheffield, Manchester, Stockport, Norwich and all over Scotland. A new network of reform organisations was created, at metropolitan, town, district and neighbourhood levels, to discuss, circulate books—especially the *Rights of Man*—and pamphlets, publish their own material, and campaign for reform. The new organisations were very different from the traditional, expensive, upper-class reform clubs. They found their members among strata of the population which had often been involved in agitation, but which had not before been organised for political action. The Vicar of Sheffield wrote in 1792 that the local Constitutional Society was composed 'of the inferior sort of manufacturers and workers'. The London Corresponding Society, the most important of all the new organisations, had among its 103 new members recruited between November 1792 and January 1793, 11 cordwainers and shoemakers, 8 tailors, 7 watchmakers, 7 weavers, 5 cabinet makers, and small numbers of frameworkers, hairdressers, dyers, hatters, bricklayers, bakers, hosiers and similar trades. The Secretary, Thomas Hardy (himself a shoemaker), wrote in March 1792 that the Society consisted mainly of 'tradesmen, mechanicks, and shopkeepers'. Many divisions of the Society had a predominantly trade, craft and artisan membership (Seaman, 1954, 29-31, 37-8). These sections of the population, many of which experienced the insecurities and 'unrest under injustice' of the early Industrial Revolution, inaugurated a new phase in what one historian calls 'the evolution of plebeian politics' (Maccoby, 1955, 93), and another 'the end to any notion of exclusiveness, of politics as the preserve of any hereditary élite or property group' (Thompson, 1963, 21).

Political movements and education

The composition of many of the new radical groups and the objectives which they set themselves dictated new forms of action. From this point education became a political weapon. One of the most important outcomes of the foundation of such organisations as the London Corresponding Society and the Sheffield Constitutional Society was an impetus to political self-education among adult, radical artisans.

The London Corresponding Society, founded to correspond with like-minded reformers elsewhere (evading a law against national political organisation), enunciated a wide political programme. Paramount, of course, was the demand for a representative Parliament, but this was a stepping stone, as the Society explained in an address in 1794, to seeing 'our liberties restored, the press free, the laws simplified, judges unbiassed, juries independent... the public better served, and the necessaries of life more within the reach of the poor' (West, 1920, 22). To achieve these ends the Society organised itself in divisions, each of which acted as a recruiting, propaganda and political education machine. At its peak periods it probably recruited 200-300 members a week, and in October 1795 had more than seventy divisions. The system of small organisational units was adopted in Sheffield in 1792, when a network of 'tythings' was created, with ten or so members in each (Seaman, 1954, 93-5). Francis Place, later to become a prominent moderate radical, was active in the London Society, and became president of its Central Committee. He describes the weekly meetings of the divisions, which elected delegates to a general committee, and which bought and discussed books: 'we had book subscriptions ... the books for which any one subscribed were read by all the members in rotation who chose to read them before they were finally consigned to the subscriber'. They met on Sunday evenings to read and discuss; the chairman for the week read aloud from a book previously read by as many people as possible. Everyone was expected to contribute to the discussion, and no one was allowed to speak a second time until everyone present had spoken once, 'and so on till the subject was exhausted' (Thale, 1972, 131).

The new organisations of the radical reformers, as well as uncountable individuals not in touch with any formal organisation, were now involved in discussion, reading, the spread of ideas, and a range of activities at a level new in English popular politics. The reformers held meetings and conventions, faced arrest and trial, held dinners and demonstrations, gave and invited lectures, planted trees of liberty, issued handbills and addresses. They circulated Paine's writings, and publicised cheap editions. In 1792, for example, the London Constitutional Society printed handbills in defence of Paine's *Rights of Man*, and sent quantities of them to related organisations elsewhere —1,200 to the Sheffield Constitutional Society, 1,200 to the Norwich Constitutional Society, and smaller numbers to Derby, Belper, Birmingham, Cambridge, and other towns (Maccoby, 1955, 55-6). The impact of such activity was

13

great and diverse. Francis Place wrote of the London Corresponding Society:

> The moral effects of the Society were considerable. It induced men to read books, instead of wasting their time in public houses, it taught them to respect themselves, and to desire to educate their children. It elevated them in their own opinions.... It gave a new stimulus to an immense number of men who had been but in too many instances incapable of any but the grossest pursuits (Thale, 1972, 198-9).

Edward Thompson has accused Place of being anxious to trace 'a sober constitutional pedigree' for the LCS, and of over-emphasising its educational activities as 'a premature Workers' Educational Association' (Thompson, 1963, 154). Although there is some element of this in Place's account it is important not to separate the Society's 'political' and 'educational' functions. The Society, in the tradition of eighteenth-century rationalism, believed that reason was bound to prevail if only it were revealed sufficiently widely. Education, for the Society's members, meant the same thing as politics. 'Information', the Society told the French National Convention in 1792, 'makes a rapid progress among us. Curiosity has taken possession of the public mind; the conjoint reign of Ignorance and Despotism passes away' (Smith, 1881, 46). The twin achievements of the radical organisations of the 1790s—which came under official attack particularly from 1794, and either weakened or disappeared—were the linking of political action and education to end the 'right of ignorance and despotism', and the elevation of a generation of common people 'in their own opinions'.

Radical responses to social and political change were also made in other ways, by other voices. At a level of more extended analysis, but one which had a profound effect in many circles, William Godwin's *Political Justice* in 1793 transmitted some of the deeper energies of eighteenth-century radical thought: 'wherever liberty, truth, justice was theme, his name was not far off' (Hazlitt, 1825, 17). Godwin's appeal was to a more limited audience than Paine's, and his impact a more intellectual one— including on writers from Wordsworth to Shelley. Godwin's *Political Justice* did not have the popular circulation and appeal of the *Rights of Man*, it was not the same kind of rallying call, but it was influential in a different way. In it Godwin propounded a theory of a just society, in which education played a central role. He mistrusted the state, however, and unlike Paine he therefore opposed the idea of government intervention in education:

> The project of a national government ought uniformly to be discouraged on account of its obvious alliance with national government. This is an alliance of a more formidable nature than the old and much contested alliance of church and state.... Government will not fail to employ it to strengthen its hands and perpetuate its institutions (Godwin, 1793, II, 302).

Education was too powerful an instrument, in Godwin's view, to be in the hands of the state, but upon its efficient and humane operation depended the creation of a just society. *Political Justice* and the *Enquirer* essays formed the most thoroughly worked out set of radical educational theories of the 1790s: they contained both a broad analysis of education's contribution to social regeneration, and a detailed discussion of questions of teaching and learning. On the latter, Godwin's central message was the need to approach education humanely and creatively: 'the first object of a system of instructing, is to give to the pupil a motive to learn. We have seen how far the established systems fail in this office' (Godwin, 1797, 79). Godwin was, of the English writers who followed the French Revolution and answered the critique of Burke, the one closest to the French philosophers of the Enlightenment, and the one who defined most sharply an approach to a radical view of education. Carrying over the ideas of the most rationalist of the Enlightenment philosophers, Helvétius, Godwin proclaimed the power of the environment (or in other words, education in its broadest sense): 'the actions and dispositions of men flow entirely from the operation of circumstances and events ... acting upon a faculty of receiving sensible impressions' (Godwin, 1793, I, 26-7). This was a doctrine which was to have far-reaching influence on future radical movements. It was a doctrine which was seen to liberate men from responsibility for their actions in a situation of adverse 'circumstances and events', and made it possible to envisage human beings behaving rationally in a rational society, through the effects of rational reform.

Others communicated similar messages, and made a parallel impact. Mary Wollstonecraft subjected Burke's attack on the French Revolution to an analysis concerned with the particular situation of women. In *The Rights of Woman* (1792) she applied the language of reason to the deprived status of women, and outlined a programme of education for boys and girls. John Thelwall, while seeing the potential in the new industrial developments, argued for a humane approach to social organisation. His ideas of social and political reform, influenced by Godwin, reached Wordsworth and Coleridge, but his popular appeal was closer to that of Paine. His biographer thought it likely that Thelwall exerted a lasting influence 'upon the educated artisans and skilled workmen to whom he addressed his speeches, for whom he wrote his books ... his teachings may have reached the democrats of the thirties and the Chartists of the forties'. The way such influences probably worked can be seen from the fact that Thelwall's manuscript diary contains 'a large number of names of artisans, shopkeepers, dissenting ministers, schoolmasters, by whom he was entertained during his tour through the provinces, in whose company he treated philosophical and political topics, and who subscribed for his books' (Cestre, 1906, 195). Thomas Holcroft, like Godwin and others of his generation, believed that reason would oust error, that

> man is happy, in proportion as he is truly informed; that his ignorance, which is the parent of his misery and vices, is not a fault, but a misfortune, which can only be remedied by infusing juster principles, and more enlightened notions into his mind ... the best and only effectual means of ameliorating the condition of mankind, is by the gentleness of instruction, by steady inquiry, and by a calm, but dauntless reliance on the progressive power of truth (Hazlitt, 1816, 140).

The main impact of the new generation of radicals was therefore in their contribution to a climate of opinion, a new value placed on reason and ideas, and a new understanding of the power of organised opinion and political action. The strands of radical explanation of the American and French Revolutions, and the development of organised responses to social and political needs in the last two decades of the eighteenth century, are the beginnings of the wider radical action of the first half of the nineteenth century.

In educational terms, the influence of the European Enlightenment and of domestic social changes also took other forms. English radicals and dissenters formed an important fraction, for example of those involved in the 'outbreak of Rousseaumania' (Stewart and McCann, 1967, 24) between the 1760s and the 1790s. Rousseau's *Émile*, published in 1762, was an important contribution to European libertarian thought, a textbook of how to educate for the development of natural virtue. A group of English followers of Rousseau expounded the ideal in books, and tried to bring up children on his model. Godwin believed that *Émile* was now 'regarded as the principal reservoir of philosophical truth as yet existing in the world'. R. L. and Maria Edgeworth and Thomas Day made outstanding contributions to the literature of the new 'educational radicalism', whose proponents included many of the enthusiastic supporters of the French Revolution (*ibid.*, 23-37; Simon, 1960, 38-56).

The social changes of the late eighteenth century also produced another important educational departure, in the Sunday school movement, not out of any radical response, but out of a sense of the dangers involved in industrial and urban change. The movement began as a simple means of providing rudimentary literary and moral education. Once the debates about the French Revolution had taken shape, however, the reaction saw the Sunday school movement as one of the English sources of subversion, given the spread of Methodist Sunday schools in particular. The Bishop of Rochester, to take an extreme example, described them as 'schools of Jacobinical rebellion and Jacobinical politics ... schools of atheism and disloyalty' (Silver, 1965, 40-2). Attacks on popular education were part of the concerted attack mounted in the mid-1790s against all forms of radical and near-radical activity, in an atmosphere in which even cautious innovation was seen as subversive.

The essential feature of this period is the emergence of strong political and social movements, with roots in dissenting and radical traditions, and establishing forms of activity, propaganda and education that were to be of vital importance to popular movements in the nineteenth century. New dimensions of discussion had been opened up, including on the nature and methods of education, human educability and the role of the state. The absence of popular political rights, and the religious and educational position of the dissenters, had been brought to the centre of discussion. The taste for ideas and books had produced the first stage of a demand for popular libraries, as well as the beginnings of collective self-help by working men in acquiring books and providing adult education. This activity must be set in the context of the new political and social awakening, due in part but not entirely to the French Revolution. Fifty years after the outbreak of the Revolution Thomas Carlyle traced the ancestry of a new generation of radicalisms:

Since the year 1789, there is now half-a-century complete; and a French Revolution not yet complete! Whosoever will look at that enormous Phenomenon may find many meanings in it, but this meaning as the ground of all: That it was a revolt of the oppressed lower classes against the oppressing or neglecting upper classes: not a French revolt only; no, a European one.... These Chartisms, Radicalisms, Reform Bill, Tithe Bill, and infinite other discrepancy, and acrid argument and jargon that there is yet to be, are *our* French Revolution (Carlyle, 1839, 26-7).

3

Middle-class radicals and education, 1800-1835

Radicalism and social class

The period with which we are concerned in this book is one which covers Edward Thompson's story of *The Making of the English Working Class* and what Asa Briggs describes as a transition from a hierarchical society to one based on 'a frank acceptance of class dividing lines' (Briggs, 1956, 65). The growth of class consciousness was relentless, and for the middle class (or middle classes as commonly described) this had, as Briggs points out, a direct political expression—the middle class had been kept out of power, but were the ones most fitted to rule.

From the turn of the century, and with continuing industrialisation, more and more issues were seen in class terms. The economic basis of class relationships was clear to observers, one typical commentary on the first half of the century being contained in a comparison of *England in 1815 and 1845*. Industrial growth provided 'the most extraordinary spectacle that the world has perhaps ever witnessed'; the aspect that was

> unparalleled in the history of the world, is the co-existence of so much suffering in one portion of the people, with so much prosperity in another; of un-

bounded private wealth, with unceasing public penury; of constant increase in the national resources, with constant diminution in the comforts of a considerable portion of the community; of the utmost freedom consistent with order, ever yet existing upon earth, with a degree of discontent which keeps the nation constantly on the verge of insurrection (Alison, 1845, 15).

In the early decades of the nineteenth century the two traditions of late eighteenth-century radicalism became identified with the two social classes whose relationships were seen to be governed by this economic reality. The middle-class radicals were heirs to the 'moderate reform' tradition, and the organisations of the working class strove to represent an independent voice of 'radical reform'. Locally and nationally the reformers often confronted each other, evolved their own organisations and styles of political and educational action, and proclaimed their objectives through different media and in different language. The fact that crises and common campaigns of one sort or another sometimes brought middle-class and working-class radicals together locally and nationally only serves to illustrate the general dichotomy—as in Leicester in 1817, when the middle-class reformers called a meeting and 'the division set by conflicting class-interests between them and the working-class radicals was for the moment smoothed over' (Patterson, 1954, 112). Although the personnel of the two camps were not always rigidly demarcated, and dialogue and joint action occurred, no smoothing over could conceal the existence in these decades of two overall radical movements, separated by class definitions and policies. Reference to middle-class and working-class radicals in this period is more than a literary shorthand, it is a distinction which points to real differences in radicalisms and in society. It is as necessary a statement about nineteenth-century politics as it is about the class-divided nature of education.

Middle-class radicalism—especially in the form of Benthamism—was basically rational, liberal and humane, attempting 'to apply the principles of Newton to the affairs of politics and of morals' (Halévy, 1928, 6). In general, however, the middle-class radicals saw the evolution of society in terms of the inevitable social and political leadership of the middle class. An article in the middle-class radical *Westminster Review* made this point clearly and in detail in its first issue in 1824. Discussing the need to reform the education of the middle class it insisted:

> Of the political and moral importance of this class, there can be but one opinion. It is the strength of the community. It contains, beyond all comparison, the greatest proportion of the intelligence, industry, and wealth of the state.... The merchant, the manufacturer, the mechanist, the chemist, the artist, those who discover new arts, those who perfect old arts, those who extend science; the men in fact who think for the rest of the world, and who really do the business of the world, are the men of this class. The people of the class below are the instruments with which they work; and those of the class above, though they may be called their governors, and may really sometimes seem to rule them, are much more often, more truly, and more completely under their control. In this country at least, it is this class which gives to the nation its character (*Westminster Review*, no. 1, 1824, 68-9).

This view was frequently reaffirmed in the early and mid-nineteenth century by Whig, liberal and radical spokesmen.

Working-class radicalism in its various forms, disillusioned at a number of critical points with middle-class reforms or policies, was based not only on a rationalist approach to the body politic and social, but also on a search for justice for an underprivileged class. It identified itself increasingly with the mass of the people, and it was without irony that the *Poor Man's Guardian*, the most vigorous of the popular radical journals of the 1830s, made this identification complete:

the Radicals are the oppressed party! The aristocracy and supporters of the present atrocious system of government—the oppressors. ... The Radicals constitute at least nine-tenths of the whole population, and these nine-tenths comprise nearly all the industry, honest mechanical skill, and creative power of the community. The other tenth is made up of all the rotten parts of the society. It consists of great lords and great ladies and gentlemen, and pensioners, and priests, and lawyers, and bankers, and great merchants (*Poor Man's Guardian*, no. 68, 1832, 546).

Throughout these early decades of the nineteenth century the analysis of society and possible reforms was made from different awarenesses of the role of different social classes. Industrialisation led to a deeper and much more explicit class separation, physical and moral, than had even been the case in pre-industrial England. The conception and provision of education were, like all aspects of society, influenced by the different angles of vision.

The break from eighteenth-century styles of political organisation and action which took place in the 1790s became complete in the first three decades of the nineteenth century. The type of radical pressure organised through the London Corresponding Society and the constitutional societies became a familiar and regular feature of early nineteenth-century politics, and it was in 'popular' or 'working-class' forms that it persisted. There were, in the shape of Luddism in the early 1810s and the agricultural workers' revolts beginning in 1830, movements which responded directly to the conditions accompanying industrial development and social change. In political terms there were attempts to organise for reform (and occasionally for revolution). The second half of the 1810s, after the end of the Napoleonic wars, saw the emergence of a new and widespread radical movement associated with popularly-based Hampden Clubs and Political Protestants. In William Cobbett they found a new spokesman, just as the radical societies had done in Paine in the 1790s (though the writings of Paine remained as vital to the new generation of radicals as they had been to the old). In the 1820s working-class radicals responded to the message of Robert Owen that it was possible to escape the evils of industrial society by co-operative organisation. The range of working-class and popular radicalisms was being extended and their focus was being sharpened. A vital element in the movement was the fight for the unrestricted publication of radical books and newspapers. The movement associated with men like Richard Carlile—the publishing and selling of free-thought and republican literature, the reprinting of the works of Tom Paine and the publication of cheap radical newspapers—was an important ingredient in the developments which led up to the first real peak of working-class radicalism in the 1830s. The underlying fact, to which all varieties of radicalism were a response, was the continued existence of an unrepresentative Parliament. The Reform Act of 1832 was an outcome of these pressures, but in a form which only led to an increase in radical agitation: the working class had found itself abandoned by some of its former middle-class allies, and derived no benefit from a reform which it had helped to secure. The *Poor Man's Guardian* explained time and again that the reform bill and the Whig ascendancy it promised were a betrayal. The bill would not 'benefit the degraded mob. It is a partial, and must be an unjust measure'. It would 'benefit none but the proud and arrogant "shopocracy".... What need have you to care which faction is in power if you have not your rights? Will the "Whigs" give you them? No more than the "Tories".' Firm, united action was needed by the down-trodden, and this was the undeviating course which 'the intelligent leaders of the "Working Classes" will take—are taking' (*Poor Man's Guardian*, no. 50, 1832, 401).

The utilitarians and education

Throughout these decades middle-class radicalism had to come to terms with such pressures from below. Aware of the uncharted hazards of a rapidly changing society, the middle-class radicals evolved a philosophy with which to approach the problems of social reform and readjustment. An influential body of radical middle-class opinion, as well as a variety of programmes, stemmed from the work of Jeremy Bentham, James Mill and their associates. Bentham 'taught his age the importance of rational criticism and systematic reform'. He 'taught Englishmen to ask if an institution was useful and efficient and conducive to human happiness' (Roberts, 1960, 29). The Benthamite doctrine of the greatest happiness of the greatest number was a facet of eighteenth-century rationalist philosophy elaborated in terms of early industrial England. It was a doctrine of utility: men sought pleasure and avoided pain, and whatever was conducive to pleasure was also useful to the individual and to society. The purpose of education, said James Mill, 'is to render the individual, as much as possible, an instrument of happiness, first to himself, and next to other beings' (Mill, 1818, 11). The Benthamites scrutinised political and social institutions through the eyes of reason. John Stuart Mill writes of James Mill's creed:

> So complete was my father's reliance on the influence of reason over the minds of mankind, whenever it is allowed to reach them, that he felt as if all would be gained if the whole population were taught to read, if all sorts of opinions were allowed to be addressed to them by word and in writing, and if by means of the suffrage they could nominate a legislature to give effect to the opinions they adopted.

J. S. Mill claims to have been the first, in 1822-3, to use the description 'utilitarian' of those thinkers 'acknowledging Utility as their standard in ethics and politics' (J. S. Mill, 1873, 67, 89). Associated with utilitarian doctrines were the views of Malthus on population and often the economic doctrines which in their extreme form proclaimed the need for 'laissez-faire', the absence of state intervention in the natural processes of, for example, industry and trade—'donothingism' as Thomas Carlyle lampooned it (Carlyle, 1843, 188). The whole of this movement, but largely the version associated with the younger generation around John Stuart Mill from the mid-1820s, also earned itself the name of 'philosophic radicalism'.

A primary objective of the utilitarians was parliamentary reform, in order to enable the manufacturing and commercial middle class to play a political role commensurate with their power in society. Their radicalism was of the nature of what Cartwright had called 'moderate reform', though it had implications which often went beyond their immediate objectives. Utilitarianism was 'a wholly adequate doctrine for the rising middle class, seeking confirmation of its growing power through reforms directed against the privileges of the aristocracy'. Its values were 'appropriate to the new methods of production' and in its early phase 'served to create the political and social institutions correspondent to the first stages of the Industrial Revolution' (Williams, 1958, 71). Middle-class pressure for factory reform, it is important to note, came not from the utilitarian reformers, but from evangelicals and Tories, men with philosophies rooted in rural, not in industrial, England.

The essential appeal of utilitarianism lay in its emphasis on a rational solution to social problems. The happiness of the people demanded it, and the individual's self-interest in a society pledged to the increase of human happiness would make it inevitable. Whatever changes took place in utilitarian doctrine, this confidence remained central to the ideas and activities of its proponents. The Benthamite philosophy attracted generations of politicians, economists and social reformers pledged to the radical reform of political and social institutions. They included thorough utilitarians like James Mill himself, the 'leading educational theoretician of the Radical movement' and prime ideologist of the middle class (Simon, 1960, 74). Associated with Bentham and Mill was Francis Place, tailor and political organiser, semi-Whig, semi-radical, 'a sort of right-hand man to Bentham and James Mill, and the moving power behind the "Philosophical Radicals"' (Leader, 1897, 27). The movement had major spokesmen in Parliament, including some who identified themselves with working-class movements, and others who were politically barely distinguishable from the Whigs. John Arthur Roebuck, a prominent figure in radical politics and educational activities in the 1830s especially, was one of the former, who described how important an influence utilitarian ideas had been on his activities (*ibid.*, 1897, ch. III). Henry (later Lord) Brougham was one of the latter. An outstanding figure in educational developments in the first half of the century, Brougham was more firmly committed to the liberal-Whig tradition than to the radicalism of the Benthamites. Nevertheless, in education particularly, he was willing to be influenced by James Mill, who, admiring Brougham's 'extraordinary energy, endeavoured to give it a good direction' (Bain, 1882, 76). Many of the philanthropists involved in social reform across this period were connected to one extent or another with the Mills and their allies. William Allen, Quaker chemist and active philanthropist, with radical ideas on a limited range of issues, published a magazine to which many of these figures contributed, played an important part in the development of popular education, and was involved with a circle of, mainly, fellow nonconformists in a number of philanthropic and reform activities. William Ellis, an important figure in education from the 1840s, considered himself a disciple of the Mills. From 1820 he was involved, like all the early Benthamite radicals in the anti-slavery movement, knew Brougham, was a friend of the Mills, and contributed to the radical journals (Robinson, 1919, 54). Though the extent of utilitarian influence has sometimes been questioned, this undoubtedly represented a widely influential body of middle-class radical thought and activity.

The boundary lines between middle-class radicalism and orthodox Whig attitudes are not easy to draw, and men like Place and Brougham moved effortlessly across them. Within the Whig-radical-utilitarian range of attitudes it was easy to be more or less moderate, seek one or another combination of limited reforms, and act within a changing network of alliances. In the context of the social disruptions seen to be caused by industrial expansion, in the presence of the serious problems of the factory and the town, it is not surprising that these alliances extended, over some issues, to Tories and evangelical Christians. The evangelical thread that runs from Wilberforce and the Clapham sect in the late eighteenth century, through the campaigns for factory reform in the 1830s, and to Shaftesbury's work for a range of social reforms, is not radical in any political sense, but it provided a momentum of social reform. Its leading members were associated at various points in time with educational campaigns, with Brougham, with Mill, with Robert Owen. Important though they are to the discussion of nineteenth-century reform activities, however, they are more remote than the utilitarians from the story of radicalism, even in its most moderate form.

The Benthamites were involved in every aspect of educational endeavour in the first half of the century, in Parliament, in the work of educational movements, in the formulation of policies. They were involved in politics and legislation, campaigns against taxes on newspapers and against corruption. A description of the middle-class campaign for the ending of the newspaper tax sums up their contribution to radical reform as

an amalgam of the several currents of thought that dominated moderate reform thinking in the early 1830s. A commitment to Benthamite utilitarianism and to the doctrines of political economy, educational reformism, the movement for free trade, demands for improvement of the postal system, and a host of concrete economic

29

grievances composed the core of this amalgam (Wiener, 1969, 22).

All utilitarian activity consisted of this amalgam, this range of interests, this mixture of objectives. Bertrand Russell has pointed out that 'most Radical movements have been inspired either by sentiments of sympathy for the oppressed, or by hatred of oppressors. In James Mill's Radicalism, neither of these is prominent' (Russell, 1934, 123). This is true of many of the utilitarian radicals: though they recognised injustice and hardship, they were moved less by sympathy than by the desire to put a rational shape on chaos. The amalgam was of currents of thought, not of feelings. James Mill, in describing early mass education in 1812, refers to 'the hideous deformity of this picture, of an ignorant and brutal people in an enlightened age and country' (Burston, 1969, 123). The question at that point was argued not in terms of oppressors and oppressed, but of a distorted, an illogical society.

Utilitarian educational policy related primarily to the development of mass education, to the reform of middle-class school and university provision. The clearest exposition of a radical-utilitarian philosophy of education is the article on 'Education' written by James Mill for the 1818 *Encyclopaedia Britannica* supplement. The central message of this article is that of the educability of the mass of the population. The crux of the argument lies in the following passage:

> The question is (and it is a question which none can exceed in magnitude), What is the degree attainable by the most numerous class? To this we have no doubt, it will, in time, very clearly appear ... that a very high degree is attainable by them.

It was desirable for the mass not to be poor and unhappy, as 'when the people are wretchedly poor, all classes are vicious, all are hateful, and all are unhappy'. People needed to be educated to ensure a well-ordered society, to ensure that they had 'a knowledge of the order of those events of nature on which our pleasures and pains depend—and the sagacity which discovers the best means for the attaining of ends'. To ask, therefore, whether the people should be educated was the same as asking whether people 'should be happy or miserable' (Mill, 1818, 29).

Adopting rationalist views from eighteenth-century France and the England of the 1790s, the utilitarians elaborated educational programmes for a developing industrial society. The range of their activities included the monitorial school, the education of infants and of adults, and the dissemination of useful knowledge—apart from their involvement with the reform of the endowed schools and of Oxford and Cambridge, and the establishment of new middle-class schools and University College, London. The movement resulted in attempts at parliamentary action, and collective and individual philanthropy, seeking to promote the extension of education in whatever ways were available.

Basic to the dissemination of utilitarian views on education was, from 1824, the *Westminster Review*, and in relation to some issues and to a small extent, the *Edinburgh Review*, a Whig journal founded in 1803, and in which, for example, Mill's and Brougham's educational enthusiasm found expression. The *Edinburgh*, in Brougham's words, devoted itself to 'the promotion of sound and liberal opinions upon all questions in Church and State' (Clive, 1957, 55). Its articles supported the monitorial system of Lancaster and the British Society, and in 1825, for example, recommended it as an economical and effective method of teaching—'enabling one master effectually to teach a greater number of children—an end which is accomplished by making the more advanced and intelligent of the children teach the rest' (*Edinburgh Review*, no. lxxxii, 1825, 321). It was common for the *Edinburgh* and for liberal-Whig and utilitarian circles to urge education as a 'rescue' operation, promoting an economical form of popular education and defending it against clerical and Tory attack. The *Westminster* was equally enthusiastic about the monitorial system, considering a system to be superior in which children taught other children, 'because from the sympathy they take in each other, they learn every thing communicable by one to the other more easily and perfectly' (*Westminster Review*, no. 1, 1824, 53). The *Westminster* was more generally critical, however, of deficiencies in popular education. It condemned the restrictive policies of some spokesmen of the Church, and played an active part in promoting educational campaigns (Aldrich, 1970, 83-113). If the utilitarians had a coherent philosophy of education, the *Westminster* played a key role in its communication and promotion.

Middle-class radicalism and popular education

On the basis of this overall position the radical and near-radical strategies for education in Parliament were constructed. While the monitorial system was establishing itself in the early decades of the century, it was clear that provision was sporadic, and that in the large towns especially the education provided either did not reach a very large proportion of poor children, or was deficient on other counts. In Parliament it was Brougham who pressed hardest for investigations, and for parliamentary pressures to be brought to bear, against the background of growing conflict between the Anglican and nonconformist communities over the provision of education, and deepening suspicions of the possibility of state intervention. Although the parliamentary radicals failed to win the national system of popular education which most of them sought, some small measure of parliamentary action was obtained in the 1810s and 1820s. In 1816 Brougham secured the appointment of a select committee to inquire into the education of the lower orders of the metropolis, in 1818 extended to cover England and Wales and then Scotland. This was followed by the appointment of a commission of inquiry into educational charities—continued in various forms until 1837. A bill presented by Brougham in 1820, aimed at a national system of education, foundered on his attempt to conciliate Church of England opinion by proposing that teachers should be members of the established Church. The radical voice in Parliament on educational matters had weakened, and was to be taken up again, as we shall see in a later chapter, by J. A. Roebuck, Thomas Wyse and others in the changed conditions of the 1830s. The most productive educational efforts of the utilitarian radicals in this period lay outside Parliament.

The utilitarians saw the Lancasterian monitorial school as a contribution to social stability, as a barrier against crime (a frequent argument used for the extension of popular education in the early nineteenth century), as an alternative to the exclusive, Anglican base of the National Society schools, and as the basis for the kind of rational society postulated by James Mill. They saw the monitorial school as a piece of labour-saving machinery on a par with the mechanical inventions of the early Industrial Revolution: the *Edinburgh Review* was not alone in using such imagery when it described how 'every boy seems to be the cog of a wheel—the whole school a perfect machine' (*Edinburgh Review*, no. xvii, 1806, 182). The machinery was used not only in the schools for the poor established by the Church of England's National Society and by the British Society—supported by dissenters and radicals: it was also adopted in grammar and public schools at different times and places in the first half of the century. The Benthamites therefore also saw the monitorial school as the device on which it would be possible to erect a complete system of education for all. When Francis Place, Mill and others helped to create the West London Lancasterian Association in 1813, to promote the spread of Lancaster's (subsequently British) schools, their motto was 'the exhilerating phrase, "Schools for All", and every now and then a note of joyful expectation breaks through the practical strain of Place's letters'. He refers to the 'health and beauty' and 'the mass of intellect' he had observed in the schools (Wallas, 1898, 97).

The radicals also had to defend the Lancasterian schools from Church attack (including in the *Westminster* and *Edinburgh* reviews). Mill published 'Schools for All, in Preference to Schools for Churchmen only' in William Allen's *Philanthropist*, as a detailed riposte to the cry of 'The Church is in danger!' The name of the Church had been 'converted into an engine of war' against undenominational education. Mill's basic argument was 'that in the opinion of the authors of the cry, Ignorance is *not* dangerous to the church ... that Knowledge *is* dangerous to the church' (Burston, 1969, 121-5). In the early decades of the nineteenth century, radicals had continually to defend educational measures against resistance and attacks from many quarters, including from the Church, which sensed itself threatened by developments not under its control, and from Tories, farmers, or anyone else afraid that an educated poor would undermine the social order.

William Hazlitt, the most consistently radical of writers, explained that:

> It is the fear of the progress of knowledge and a *Reading Public*, that has produced all the fuss and bustle and cant about Bell and Lancaster's plans ... and that when it was impossible to prevent our reading something, made the Church and State so anxious to provide us with the sort of food for our stomachs, which they thought best (Hazlitt, 1819, 325).

Manchester radical Rowland Detrosier was asked by the proprietor of a large firm whether he knew someone who would take a job as a porter: 'I don't want one of your intellectuals,' said the inquirer, 'I want a man that will work and take his glass of ale, I'll think for him' (Williams, 1965, 22). The middle-class radicals were well aware of the resistance to be overcome.

The search for widely applicable methods of education also produced the ultra-rationalist 'chrestomathic' proposals of Bentham himself. His *Chrestomathia* (1816) was an attempt to apply monitorial-type methods to education of a higher type. Mill, Place and others were involved in the scheme to establish a school based on the ideas Bentham elaborated, consisting of a highly organised curriculum, excluding classical learning and establishing a progression based on the principle of utility, and including science. As early as 1769 Bentham had devised an encyclopedic plan of human knowledge, one which he now made, together with ideas on pedagogy and school design related to monitorial developments, the basis of his detailed proposals. Although the plan fell through it illustrated a continuing concern to explore the possibilities of improving the curriculum and pedagogy of middle-class schools (Bain, 1882, 86-8; Halévy, 1928, 286-8; Simon, 1960, 79-82).

Middle-class radicals were also among those who patronised infant schools on the model of Robert Owen's infant school at New Lanark. The sponsors of the first infant school opened in London, in 1819, included Brougham and James Mill (and the first teacher was obtained from the New Lanark school). Owen's social and educational reforms at New Lanark were well known in this period. From 1814 his partners at the mills included Bentham and William Allen, and he knew most of the leading London utilitarians. There was throughout this period a constant search for new ideas and models, in Britain and on the Continent, resulting in the opening of schools of a more or less experimental kind. The schools at Hill Top and Hazelwood, in Birmingham, and at Bruce Castle, Tottenham, all associated with the family of Thomas Wright Hill, were in the tradition of earlier experiments, but with a programme defined in the light of later developments. The Hills were catering for middle-class children, but like other radicals, including the 'chrestomathic' group, they were interested in the implications of the monitorial system. They saw that the monitorial school was 'admirably adapted to answer its purpose: but it has essential defects, which render it unfit for general adoption'. They wanted to teach children 'to *think* as well as act', and to encourage self-government and responsible behaviour: 'the principle of our government is to leave, as much as possible, all power in the hands of the boys themselves' (Hill, 1822, 1, 124-5). J. A. Roebuck, believing that religion ought to play no part in education, opened a model school in Bath to illustrate his principles (Leader, 1897, 57). William Allen, in addition to his treasureship of the British Society and his connection with New Lanark, established an agricultural colony and a school of industry at Lindfield (Salmon,

1905, 19). The middle-class radicals were never far from educational plans and activities.

The grammar and public schools

The radical attack on the endowed grammar and public schools, as on the ancient universities, was directed largely at their failure to meet modern educational needs, and at what the radicals saw as the long-standing diversion of their endowments away from the poor. Outspoken attacks on the classical curriculum and pedagogy of the endowed schools were made in the *Edinburgh* and *Westminster* reviews, against a background of increasing awareness of the decrepitude and inefficiency of many of the grammar and public schools. Nicholas Carlisle's *Concise Description of the Endowed Grammar Schools* (1818) produced a factual picture of the large number of schools providing sinecures, with illiterate teachers, without pupils, neglected, decayed or closed. In the same year Brougham published *A Letter to Sir Samuel Romilly* describing the abuse of charities on which schools were based, and pointing out that endowments intended for the education of the poor were often not being used for that purpose (New, 1961, 218). The charity commissioners appointed as a result of Brougham's efforts reported between 1819 and 1837, and the legal action that followed removed some of the abuses. But the classical curriculum and traditional routines remained basic to the operation of the public schools and better grammar schools. Legal restrictions on the application of endowments for the teaching of modern subjects acted as a constraint until 1840, and the radical response was one of sustained criticism of the schools and efforts to create alternatives. The Benthamites kept up a critique of the schools, on the grounds that, in James

Mill's words, 'an institution for education which is hostile to progression, is ... the most preposterous, and vicious thing, which the mind of man can conceive' (Mill, 1818, 31). Others joined in the attack. Thomas Wyse, MP, complained in the 1830s that children in grammar schools were 'fed with the dry husks of ancient learning, when they should be taking sound and substantial food from the great treasury of modern discovery' (Wyse, 1837, 59-60), and in the 1840s a pamphleteer expressed with great clarity a viewpoint often heard in earlier decades:

> The country would be better without its endowed public schools. Servility and tyranny are perpetuated there. The nation may justly claim all these endowments, as they have been perverted from their original purpose. They were intended for the children of the poor, and they have been appropriated to the sons of the rich (Spencer, 1843, 13).

The alternative 'secondary' education supported by many radicals was the proprietary school, financed as a joint-stock company, often by like-minded religious, commercial or other circles (Simon, 1960, 115-25). Their outstanding merit was that, being free of the restrictions placed on charitable endowments, they could develop modern curricula seen as suitable for the communities in which they were established. From 1825 such schools appeared in many towns, particularly growing commercial centres. The model was University College School, London, founded by a group which included James Mill and Brougham. From 1831 it developed a wide curriculum (including science, mathematics and social science), without compulsory subjects, and with new approaches to discipline—not using the corporal punishment virtually universal in the endowed schools (Bellot, 1929, 169-71;

Felkin, 1909, 7-8). Other schools which followed often expressed a debt to UCS and to its Benthamite philosophy. The Leicester Proprietary School, opened in 1837, 'declared its principles—liberal, unsectarian, and utilitarian—to be those of Brougham; and its model to be University College School (Patterson, 1954, 243).

The universities

Mill, Brougham and other Benthamites, radicals and liberals, attacked the curriculum, organisation, finances, and teaching at Oxford and Cambridge on a similar basis to that of their attack on the endowed schools, and in the same way they aimed both at reform of what existed and the creation of an alternative. The late eighteenth century had seen strong attacks on the narrow classical learning, ineffectiveness and torpitude of the two universities. To attacks on their 'medievalism' was now added the voice of the dissenters, whose demand for 'entry into what they described as "national universities" had triumphed over their suspicion that they were better off without it' (Ward, 1965, 81). James Mill described European universities in general as 'enemies of all innovation' (Mill, 1818, 31). The *Edinburgh Review* attacked the universities in 1808, and again in a famous series of articles on Oxford in 1831. Between these dates there was mounting radical criticism of the exclusive Anglican and classical nature of the universities. As liberal-Whig Sydney Smith put it: 'an infinite quantity of talent is annually destroyed in the Universities of England by the miserable jealousy and littleness of ecclesiastical instructors' (Smith, 1810, 268). In Parliament and in print the demands for reform and for the removal of the religious tests came into full flood in the 1830s, though not until 1850 was a commission appointed to inquire into the affairs of Oxford and Cambridge.

A major success for the radicals, Whigs and dissenters was the foundation of what was intended to be London University, and became University College, London. The aim of the project, said Thomas Campbell, one of its principal founders, was that 'of effectively and multifariously teaching, examining, exercising, and rewarding with honours in the liberal arts and sciences, the youth of our middling rich people, between the age of 15 or 16 and 20, or later if you please' (Bellot, 1929, 52). The new college opened in 1828 and together with the rival Church establishment, King's College, became the University of London in 1836. University College had no religious tests, and had a wide curriculum in science and medicine, ancient and modern languages, engineering and law. The new institution was to be liberal, utilitarian and modern. The first Council embraced the interest networks we have seen at work in other education contexts—Brougham and liberal-Whigs, Mill and Utilitarians, men who had been involved with Lancaster, and others—including George Birkbeck, associated with the mechanics' institutes. The fact that the wider spectrum of representatives included Jews, Catholics and evangelicals does not detract from the importance of the project as a major focus for the older generation of utilitarians.

Adult education

From 1823 adult education became another such focus. The London Mechanics' Institute was launched in that year, to instruct members 'in the arts they practise, and in other branches of scientific and useful knowledge' (Tylecote, 1957, 19). The originators included Thomas

Hodgskin, critic of the utilitarian economists and drawing support from radical artisans. Hodgskin's view was that the institutes would 'teach men the moral as well as the physical sciences.... No Holy Alliance can put down the quiet insurrection by which knowledge will subvert whatever is not founded in justice and truth' (Hodgskin, 1825, 110-11). The movement came to be dominated, however, by middle-class patrons with more limited objectives; George Birkbeck, Place, Brougham and others moulded the movement in such a way as to deprive it of working-class leadership. The government of the individual institutes tended to consist of middle-class patrons, and the moral or political science which Hodgskin hoped to see taught was largely barred from the curriculum, in London and elsewhere. Probably the most useful function served by the institutes was through their libraries, and in some cases they created day schools on their premises. At Liverpool there were not only schools for boys and girls, but, unusually, classes for female teachers run by the secretary, a library, a museum and evening classes for adults (Meiklejohn, 1883, 24-7). The institutes were generally held in suspicion by the Tory and High Church party, as breeding grounds for disaffection, but they were also distrusted by many working men, given the middle-class patronage of most of them, and restrictions on subjects for lecturing, library provision and debate. A retrospective comment in 1849 by Thomas Cooper, one of the Chartist leaders, explains the attitude of many working men to the institutes in this period of growing political awareness and action:

In many instances, the subscription was beyond the means of the poverty-stricken artisan; in all, the rules restricting political and theological enquiry and discussion, and forbidding Sunday reading in the book-room, were irksome; and the undue influence of patrons and annual subscribers was felt as a tyranny. Numerous independent societies of working-men have thus sprung up (*Plain Speaker*, vol. I, no. 19, 1848, 148).

What these 'independent societies' were we shall see in later chapters. The 'irksome' restrictions of the institutes were matched by restrictions placed on the parallel Society for the Diffusion of Useful Knowledge. This society, founded in 1827, had Brougham and Mill on its London committee, as well as many others connected with the foundation of University College—including Leonard Horner, the first Warden. The prospectus of the society stated its object to be 'the imparting of useful information to all classes of the community, particularly to such as are unable to avail themselves of experienced teachers, or may prefer learning by themselves' (SDUK, 1829, 17). These were the beginnings of the middle-class patronage of working-class self-help, later made famous by Samuel Smiles, and though some of the books published cheaply by the society were useful technical manuals, most of its publications provoked contempt among working-class radicals. In 1832 the *Poor Man's Guardian*, in an attack on Brougham, described the SDUK as 'the disgusting society at which he is the head'. The society, 'under the mask of a liberal diffusion of really useful information, has spread abroad more canting, lying, mischievous trash, than, perhaps, any other society that ever existed'. The society's weekly *Penny Magazine* was described by the *Poor Man's Guardian* in the same year as 'containing a pack of nonsensical tittle tattle, about forks and spoons, and smock frocks, bridges, waterfalls, and a thousand other things, no doubt entertaining enough, but to the poor and ignorant, utterly useless' (*Poor Man's Guardian*, no. 60, 1832, 486; no. 70, 1832, 565). The approach of some of the middle-class radicals and their allies to the mechanics' institutes and to the useful knowledge movement demonstrates the sharp split, most visible in the 1830s, between their philosophy of social reform and social control, and the reform activities of the independent working-class movement.

The middle-class radicals of these decades were engaged in other efforts to provide a cheap press and cheap books. Charles Knight, a publisher involved in the useful knowledge movement, looked back from 1864 at the 'vast changes in the social condition of the people, in the progress of which elementary education and popular literature have been amongst the most efficient instruments of amelioration' (Knight, 1864, I, iv). The expansion of mass education was accompanied by the development of the *Penny Magazine*, the cheap serial encyclopedia, the woodcut illustration, 'useful knowledge' about industrial and scientific processes—and less often about economics and politics. The middle-class radical patron, lecturer, campaigner, journalist and publisher played central parts in these developments. Cheap publications, untaxed newspapers— these were objectives crucial to both middle-class and working-class radicals, though with differing emphases. In the 1830s the middle-class radicals organised, campaigned, negotiated, to try to secure the repeal of the 'taxes on knowledge', but stopped far short of the violations of the stamp laws deliberately committed by the unstamped working-class radical press. One historian of the period describes the middle-class radical campaign as one

to introduce motions in Parliament, backed by a 'pressure from without' which they had created by means of petitions, public meetings, and deputations.... The middle-class radicals hoped that cheap newspapers would

imbue the working classes with truer notions of order-
liness, sobriety, and political economy ... would teach
working men what the laws were and why they should
be obeyed ... the middle-class radicals wanted the repeal
of the duties to break the monopoly of the existing pro-
prietors and to purify the stamped press by widening its
readership ... a cheap press was essential if middle-class
ideas were to gain currency among working men.

Working-class radicals, on the other hand, expected a
cheap press to 'teach the working man the dignity of his
class', show him 'that the laws were bad and help to
organise and unify the working class' (Hollis, 1970, 10-12).
Another account explains that 'the working-class ideological spectrum involved a much greater intensity of
feeling and emotion and a deeper personalization of the
newspaper issue ... for the committed amongst the
laborers, newspaper repeal took on near-messianic quality'
(Wiener, 1969, 115). It is important, before we turn to
the nature of working-class radicalism in the early nineteenth century, to stress that even on this issue, of great
importance to reformers of all kinds, class divisions were
deep.

The middle class and reform

Middle-class radicalism was not merely a body of ideas,
concerned exclusively with education, and based solely on
utilitarian philosophies. It is true, as John Stuart Mill
pointed out, that the *Westminster Review* (though we
could also add other, more informal networks) gave Benthamism 'a status, in the arena of opinion and discussion
... out of all proportion to the number of its adherents'
(J. S. Mill, 1873, 82). Utilitarian or 'philosophic' radicalism

is stressed here because it articulated most fully the social programme that was implied by any middle-class demands for reform. Middle-class radicalism did not operate in a vacuum. The growing industrial and commercial power of the middle class constantly underlay its demand for a share in political power. It also had to respond to the more vigorous demands expressed in the various phases of the working-class radical movement. Major Cartwright, pursuing a 'substantial and radical reform in the representation of the people' (Cartwright, 1812, 5-6), founded the Hampden Club together with Sir Francis Burdett in 1812, but the radical Hampden Clubs which mushroomed in 1816 had a subscription not of £2 a year, but of 1d. a week, and with a fuller suffrage demand than that of 1812 (Halévy, 1926, 11-14). From this point on it was a more popular, more working-class form of radicalism that made the running, through popular organisations of the type of the Hampden Clubs of 1816-17 and the Political Protestants of 1818. Inside and outside Parliament the middle-class radicals were never a coherent party, and they found themselves having to define a position which demarcated them from the working-class radicals, and also from the Whigs, with whom their links became increasingly tenuous. The reform struggles leading up to 1832 sharpened these demarcation lines. In 1831 Brougham was reasserting a Whig-utilitarian view we have seen earlier: 'By the People, I mean the middle classes, the wealth and intelligence of the country, the glory of the British name' (Briggs, 1956, 69). In 1832 he became identified with the continuation of the stamp duties under the reformed Parliament. With the Whig refusal to countenance any further measure of reform Whig-radical ties were broken. The French Revolution of 1830 also pushed many middle-class radicals into a new degree of hostility to the British aristocracy clinging to parliamentary power. Their position was complicated by the fact that anti-radical opinion often indiscriminately attacked all radicals, reformers and dissenters as revolutionaries and scoundrels (Hobsbawm and Rudé, 1969, 215-16), whilst working-class movements in the early 1830s often looked suspiciously on their middle-class allies.

In education outstandingly the middle-class radicals felt at home. From the mid-1830s they found new ways of organising their educational efforts, in the collection of information, conducting of investigations, and exercising of pressure, with the intention of improving educational provision. It was said by a sympathiser that 'our educators are, after all, the best reformers, and doing the best for their country, whether they intend so or not' (Bamford, 1893, II, 15). Faced with acute social problems and increasing popular agitation in the 1830s, for middle-class reformers 'doing the best for their country' often meant using education as a weapon with which to protect the social order. In different contexts and at different times middle-class reformers saw the school as a means of reducing crime and pauperism, of combating agitation which could trade on 'the superstition of an ignorant population' (Kay-Shuttleworth, 1862, 232), and of promoting social cohesion. Motives such as these were interwound with the most rational, liberal and philanthropic aims of the middle-class radicals, and where the emphasis lay in their pronouncements was governed by their perception of prevalent social tensions.

4

Working-class radicalism and education, 1800-1835

The English working class

There have always been economic, occupational, status and regional differences within the working class. In the early nineteenth century, at the bottom of the hierarchy, or even below it, were the poor, the unemployed, those for whom the Poor Law and charity were a constant reality. One of the earliest historical treatments of working-class conditions, in 1867, explained that the terms 'working class' and 'working men' would be taken 'in their every-day acceptation, as meaning those who work, chiefly with their muscles, for wages, and maintain themselves thereby'. By this definition those not regularly in work, or with low earning capacity, were not of the working class, and the book did not intend to deal with 'the poor', that is, 'those who may work, but cannot thereby habitually maintain themselves, otherwise than by an occasional glimpse at some of their efforts to raise themselves into the true working class' (Ludlow and Jones, 1867, 3). At the top of the working-class hierarchy were highly skilled craftsmen, often distinguished from other workers by only slight gradations of status and style of life, political and cultural consciousness. Evidence to a parliamentary commission showed:

Even the fine spinners, who were the best paid, were only distinguished from the rest by their extravagant riotousness. Topics of conversation were limited; power to converse rationally was possessed by few; the noise of the factory was unfavourable to the exchange of ideas. Ignorant themselves, what wonder if they cared little to educate their children? (*ibid.*, 13-14).

Better paid craftsmen in non-factory occupations might suffer from other disadvantages, but often were far more amenable to education, ideas and radical politics—all still as inter-woven as in the activities of the London Corresponding Society. It was often the better paid craftsmen who gave the impetus to radical movements and organisations. The first objective defined for the London Working Men's Association in 1836—the first step towards the Chartist movement—was 'to draw into one bond of unity the intelligent and influential portion of the working classes in town and country' (Lovett, 1876, 94). It was men such as these who responded to arguments in support of political rights, which, in the language of 1837, 'necessarily stimulate men to enquiry—give self-respect' (*ibid.*, 120). In spite of these economic and social differences, working-class conditions and responses were parallel enough to provide, at critical moments of social and political change particularly, a sense of the reality of class. When Engels in 1844 described the culture, the literature, the periodicals and pamphlets, and the radicalism of the working class, he was describing a class which was conscious of its general role within a set of definable social and economic relationships. He wrote:

The workers are conscious of the fact that they form a separate class, and have their own interests, policies, and points of view, which are opposed to those of the capitalist property owners. Above all they are conscious of the fact that on their shoulders rests the real power of the nation and the hope of its future progress (Engels, 1845, 273).

It would be wrong to oversimplify the working-class situation and outlook in the first three decades of the century. It has rightly been pointed out that it is difficult to grasp 'in its entirety the pattern of British proletarian endeavor during the ten years preceding Queen Victoria's accession. The movement was so extensive, the objectives were so diverse, and the incidence of the various appeals was often so localized' that the story is difficult to disentangle (as it is also to some degree for the previous two decades). Participants 'frequently complained of a chronic lack of unity', and men moved in and out of a whole variety of movements with overlapping objectives and support (Driver, 1946, 261). Yet it is possible even in this period to detect prevalent and unifying aspects of a new working-class consciousness. Responses to economic crises of early industrialisation were often widely uniform. Similar political and social ideas were often widely held. An underlying sense of social, economic and political injustice can be seen at work in the period following the Napoleonic wars, preceding the passing of the Reform Act of 1832, and in agitation against the reform of the Poor Law in 1834. The 1820s have been described as ' "the decade of silent insurrection", when a specifically working-class consciousness was developing, in education, political action, trade organisation, even cultural aspiration' (Williams, 1965, 4). Working men of all kinds shared the consciousness of being socially separate, unenfranchised, similarly vulnerable.

They therefore shared a growing sense of identity, a widely disseminated radical culture. They established traditions of self-education, and continued in many forms the tradition of mutual improvement, and organisations based in the democratic structure of the class meeting. The Chartist movement and its predecessors 'gave to the humblest the opportunity of raising his voice in public meeting, an opportunity that was embraced with avidity': the early Chartist movement 'was quite an era in working-class oratory' (Gammage, 1854, 17). The radical press taught and itself represented a common set of ideals, a common sense of power. In 1840 the *Northern Star* was described as 'only the consequence of an advance made by the unenfranchised in combination and power ... the *Northern Star* is a bond of union'. The unenfranchised 'are learning the art of exercising their combined power by practice' (*Tait's Edinburgh Magazine*, vol. VII, 1840, 811). Working-class cultural and political consciousness had by the 1830s shown the existence of a diverse but identifiable 'British proletarian endeavor'—with educational ideals and activities playing an important role.

Working-class politics and education

The ideals of working-class radical movements throughout these decades were constructed on the basis of a sense of the value and power of knowledge, human perfectibility, the possibility of rapid solutions to the ills of early industrial society. All working-class movements laid great emphasis on the press as the disseminator of knowledge and ideas—and hence the profoundly educative purposes of the press itself and of the fight to remove the taxes on newspapers. The motto of the Brighton *Co-operator* read:

Knowledge and union are power:
Power, directed by knowledge, is happiness:
Happiness is the end of creation.

That of the *Poor Man's Guardian* was 'Knowledge is power'.
The *Co-operator*, like Robert Owen and countless others,
attacked ignorance as the enemy. In a pungent passage in
1828, for example, it ascribed current social evils to ignorance: 'We are born ignorant—brought up ignorant—we
live and die ignorant. We are like men groping in thick
darkness.' The first and last step towards effective co-
operation was to remove such ignorance (*Co-operator*, no.
1, 1828, 3). Rowland Detrosier persistently argued that
ignorance was the cause of injustice. Working men had
achieved some unity, but it had not brought results: 'in
the pride of half knowledge the working men of this
country have united, and they have expected the consequences of wisdom from the operations of comparative
ignorance' (Detrosier, 1831, 2). As he also explained elsewhere, in language strongly reminiscent of the 1790s: 'man
is progressive, and human perfectibility is not a chimera;
but that perfectibility cannot be attained until the great
mass of our population is morally and politically free'
(Detrosier, 1834, 246). Working-class Owenites saw in the
idea of co-operative communities the means of achieving
not only better material conditions, but also new human
relations and education. 'The regular acquisition of knowledge', wrote the first working-class Owenite newspaper,
on the subject of people in communities, 'and progress in
intelligence, will go on, without interruption, for many
years'—in fact, throughout the individual's lifetime
(*Economist*, no. 9, 1821, 139).

Early working-class radical ideals therefore contained
strong commitments to political, cultural and educational

advance. The spirit of such radical ideals was often, especially in the early decades, strongly millenarian or messianic. There was a sense that knowledge (like union, co-operation, parliamentary reform, phrenology, or a host of other instruments) could bring immediate social improvements. Robert Owen in the 1810s was given to pronouncements about the dawning of a new era. Change was seen as irresistible once knowledge was abroad. In 1818 Owen told the governments of Europe and America that 'the dominion of ignorance, of fraud, and of violence, is also on the point of terminating' (Owen, 1818, 211). The *Co-operator* announced that as soon as men

> acquire enough knowledge to understand a better system, they will begin to act upon it; and then farewell to poverty and distress ... farewell to all anxiety about work, health and sickness, wife and children, and even about death itself, so far as it affects the comfort and independence of a family (*Co-operator*, no. 5, 1828, 3).

The distress and difficulties of early industrial Britain led to a search for panaceas and certainties. For radical working-class movements the central ones—though they were not universally shared—were essential rights and freedoms, major social and industrial reforms, the ability to use the vital instrument of knowledge.

Across the first three decades of the nineteenth century independent working-class activity changed its dominant emphasis at a number of points. In the 1810s it was concerned centrally with agitation for political reform, whilst in the 1820s, mainly under the impact of Robert Owen, it became increasingly concerned with possibilities of social reorganisation. The 1830s saw swiftly changing emphases on alternative, and sometimes parallel or linked social and political objectives. From 1825, with the repeal of the

Combination Laws, trade-union organisation and activity played a fluctuating part.

Popular radicalism and its organisations

A new lease of life for popular radicalism came after the end of the wars, with the spread of Hampden Clubs, charging a minimal subscription and addressing their propaganda among others to the factory workers (Halévy, 1926, 13-14). The new burst of reform was accompanied by the establishment of secular evening and Sunday schools. At Middleton, near Manchester, the Hampden Club raised enough funds at a penny a week to rent a disused chapel, which it 'threw open for the religious worship of all sects and parties, and there we held our meetings on the evenings of Monday and Saturday in each week' (Bamford, 1893, II, 12). The leading figures of the Leicester Hampden Club were 'small tradesmen or superior artisans', and in November 1816 it had more than 500 members (Patterson, 1954, 107-8). In 1818 the radical movement also produced, starting in Hull, the Political Protestants, whose promoters declared their belief 'that political ignorance has been the cause of our national misery and degradation', and called for 'a firm and extensive Union of the people to promote and diffuse a correct knowledge of our immediate rights' (Wearmouth, 1937, 64-5). By the early 1820s the radical movement had subsided.

The radical popular and working-class movements of this period continued in many ways the earlier traditions. They also discussed Tom Paine and other radical literature; they also organised themselves into classes for political discussion and education. From the battles of the 1810s also emerged the fight against restrictions on the press and publications; Richard Carlile—a central figure in the fight from this point—provided radicalism with a great deal of its literature and energy, expressing a vigorous republicanism, and a Painite condemnation of monarchy and priestcraft. He and many of the sellers of his publications went to gaol for the right to publish and sell what the law called seditious and blasphemous libel. A new momentum of working-class and popular journalism was carried forward by papers like Wooler's *Black Dwarf* and Cobbett's *Register*. In Leeds James Watson in 1818 had his first encounter with radicalism in this context:

> I saw at the corner of Union Court a bill, which stated that the Radical Reformers held their meetings in a room in that court. Curiosity prompted me to go and hear what was going on. I found them reading Wooler's *Black Dwarf*, Carlile's *Republican*, and Cobbett's *Register*. I remembered my mother being in the habit of reading Cobbett's *Register* (Linton, 1879, 17).

The role of William Cobbett in this new generation of radical reformers was crucial. Many who could barely read sharpened their literacy on Cobbett's *Register*, or listened to their more literate brethren reading it aloud in the inn or the open air. His popular support was immense. He spoke with a political directness which made him the champion of popular radicalism, as fundamental to the discussions of the Hampden and other radical clubs of the 1810s as Paine had been to those of the 1790s. One by no means sympathetic contemporary commented on Cobbett's production of the famous twopenny *Register* in 1816:

> The 'Register' in November, 1816, became a twopenny publication. It was soon equally to be found in the mechanics' club-room of the North and in the village ale-house of the South. Gaping rustics would eagerly

listen to some youngster who had learnt to read since the days of Bell and Lancaster, as he poured forth the racy English, in which there were no fine words or inverted sentences (Knight, 1864, I, 188).

Cobbett, political radicalism of various shades, the Hampden Clubs and Political Protestants—these were the energies which built across from the earlier generation of radical reformers to the more thoroughly working-class activities of the 1830s.

The Political Protestants demonstrated most clearly the class meeting basis of much popular organisation. The Hull organisation decided to meet once a week in classes of not more than twenty, and 'to subscribe one penny each, for the purpose of purchasing such means of information as may be required'. The model was widely copied, and Protestant Unions and similar reform organisations adopted this kind of organisational basis all over the North of England, Midlands, London and elsewhere. The Stockport Political Society in 1819 was meeting in classes once a week to read Cobbett, the *Black Dwarf* 'and other works, calculated to diffuse political knowledge'—and a radical women's society was also created in Stockport (Wearmouth, 1948, 31-42). Women played a significant part in many local radical organisations, and Stockport was not the only town to have an active women's radical organisation. A West Riding Chartist wrote of the period after the Peterloo massacre in 1819 that the women of his village 'were not behind the men in their love for liberty, for I have heard my mother tell of their having regular meetings and lectures at the house of Thomas Washington, a shoemaker', and the shoemaker's wife marched with other women in procession, 'carrying the cap of liberty on the top of a pole' (Wilson, 1887, 1).

By the 1810s and 1820s working-class movements were operating in a situation of continuing and intense social problems, especially in the northern urban and industrial areas. The search for political solutions remained basic to the working-class response, but other aspects of that response were to grow in intensity; alternative lines of radical advance were to be sought. The essential element in working-class consciousness from this point onwards was the sense of autonomy—the pursuit of independent activities and solutions, suspicion of middle-class patronage, in education as well as in politics. One expression of this consciousness was the conflict that simmered in many mechanics' institutions over middle-class and aristocratic patronage, and resulting bans on political discussion and political literature in their libraries. It was a conflict which in a small number of places also led to the establishment of break-away institutes, and to support for alternative forms of working men's and radical meeting places.

Owen, Owenism and education

Another expression of this consciousness was the adoption of the social programme of Robert Owen by working men, and the creation of working-class Owenite organisations. Owen, in ways far removed from those of Cobbett, was to help working men to define their ideals in opposition to the middle class and its values, in opposition to the in-humane quality of urban, industrial life on the basis of which the middle class was itself seeking to establish political as well as economic power.

Owen's central and consistent message was that 'man's character is formed for and not by him'. By banishing ignorance and establishing the power of truth a rational society would ensue. His hypothesis about character led him to postulate that once society realised this fact, it could—and would—make rational changes. An educational and social millennium was at hand. The reign of ignorance, he wrote in *A New View of Society*, 'rapidly approaches to dissolution ... the knowledge of the existing errors is not only possessed by the learned and reflecting, but it is spreading far and wide throughout society' (Silver, 1969, 108). Owen went on from the late 1810s to propose the organisation of co-operative communities, at first as a palliative for social and economic problems, and then as the basis for the reorganisation of the whole of society. His proposals were always rooted in a total view of human perfectibility, the social and human potential of new industrial and technical progress if rationally used. Owen rejected political action and propounded a view of social progress which contained a rounded vision of education and human happiness. His writings abound in such programmes and visions:

> The overwhelming power, which, through the progress of knowledge, may be now obtained, by the external circumstances under the control of society, to form the general character of the human race, will become evident to all, and in consequence, no child will be permitted to grow up in ignorance, in superstition, or with inferior dispositions or habits; or without a knowledge of his own organization, of its laws, of the laws of nature generally, of the useful sciences, and of the practical arts of life.

Ignorance and the poverty which it produced would, under Owen's rational system of society, 'be known only, in the history of the past, or of the irrational period of human existence' (Owen, 1836, xx-xxii). His confidence in human nature and the power of education took him beyond what

he considered the narrow schemes of Bell and Lancaster
(though he gave financial support to both). His experience
at New Lanark led him to formulate—especially in terms
of the infant school—what has been called 'the first important attempt made in this country to base a practical
scheme of education on an original study of the child'
(Dobbs, 1919, 167).

In the first quarter of the nineteenth century Owen
remodelled New Lanark as an industrial community, along
lines which he described in *A New View of Society*. New
Lanark became Owen's qualification to speak and to be
heard. The humane view of children embodied in the
schools, the quality of the teachers he chose and trained,
his stress on the importance of the infant school, of play
and the need for the children to be healthy and 'active,
cheerful, and happy' (Select Committee, 1816, 240), made
New Lanark and Owen household names. Although Owen's
message was directed primarily to the influential, it was
responded to most directly in the 1820s by the radical
working class. *A New View*, published in 1816, 'may be
regarded as the starting point of modern Socialism' (Wallas,
1898, 63).

The Owenite movement reached a high-water mark of
popular activity in the early 1830s. The working-class
Owenites of the early 1820s had absorbed Owen's message
of social regeneration through co-operative organisation.
They began to try to form communities, or to plan for
them. They tried to form producers' co-operatives and
organisations to promote co-operative knowledge. They
published newspapers and publicised the work of Owen
and other advocates of co-operation. Everywhere, Owen's
own commitment to education was reflected in the activities of the co-operators. The Rules adopted by the London
Co-operative Society in 1825, for example, include one

which outlined as objectives to 'diffuse all the information on social arrangements ... occasional meetings for lectures and discussion ... by publications of the Society ... periodical publications ... weekly meetings of the Society ... social meetings of the members' (*Rules*, 1825, 3). The early newspapers of the co-operators discussed New Lanark and other pioneering educational ventures, and underlined the importance both of the spread of co-operative knowledge among adults, and the improved education of their children, as vital weapons for social advance. With the rapid spread of Owenite organisations in the early 1830s—including 'labour exchanges' and Owenite influence in trade unions—one of the two peaks of popular educational activity was reached (the other was to be the Chartist movement). The journals of the movement were preoccupied with education, and co-operative and related activities were widespread.

The Owenite press at the end of the 1820s and in the early 1830s detailed the progress of the movement. A section of the *Birmingham Co-operative Herald*, for example, was always devoted to the progress of the movement. In April 1829 this meant purely the work of the Birmingham Co-operative Society, but subsequent issues gave details of co-operative trading and production ventures elsewhere in the Midlands, including Leicestershire (stocking production), Kidderminster and Belper (trading—including in the latter case killing their own meat), Loughborough, Walsall and elsewhere. It reported speeches and writings on co-operation, including Owen's, and took up among other educational proposals one from Liverpool to establish a co-operative college where 'pupils might live in community'. Infant education was enthusiastically advocated: 'commenced by the benevolent Owen, at New Lanark, and now so extensively diffused through the medium of infant schools over the land', it was 'spreading its benefits far and wide' (*Birmingham Co-operative Herald*, no. 17, 1830, 70). Co-operators opened schools, including evening and Sunday schools. Owenite dockers in Liverpool established a library, Owenite builders in Birmingham and nationally wrote educational activities into their consti-tutions, Owenite congresses discussed educational develop-ments. Rowland Detrosier, at the second co-operative con-gress, in 1831, 'although he could hardly consider himself a Co-operative Missionary, felt he was engaged in the same noble employment, the improvement of men's minds'. A resolution of the same congress urged societies to estab-lish schools of industry and 'to apply a portion of their sub-scriptions and profits of trade, to the maintenance of proper teachers in the said schools' (Co-operative Con-gresses, 1831-2, 6, 24). When the Birmingham builders' union decided in 1833 to build a guildhall their aims included : 'to provide for themselves a school of instruction in all the branches of the art of building; also a good, sound and practical education for their children'. The Grand National Guild of Builders stated that one of their objects was 'to educate both adults and children'. The Society for National Regeneration, created in 1833 by Owen, factory reformer John Fielden and others to campaign for an eight-hour day, also included the establishment of schools among its aims. A meeting in Manchester to set up a branch of this society called on existing day and Sunday schools to open their school rooms to the working class two hours a day, and appealed for volunteers 'to assist in promoting their education when time for such purposes has been secured to them' (Morris, 1952, 203, 207, 871, 875).

Throughout this period there was a tension, at some points no more than a rivalry, at others a more open hos-tility, between the Owenites and the radical political reformers. There was often an overlap or an interchange of membership. After the peak of Owenite activity in 1833-4 Owenism became a more restricted, propagandist movement, with meeting places often called Halls of Science, and still strongly committed to the cause of education—as well as to what from this point was called its 'socialism', and its secularism. The Owenite legacy of educational activity was also taken over, as we shall see, by a new style of co-operative trading movement which became widespread after the establishment of the Rochdale Pioneers' store in 1844.

The Owenite interest in communities, co-operation and education was an alternative to political action; it was radical in the direction of its energies, not in the political sense we have used for earlier movements. Owen and his working-class followers rapidly established an ideal of education which surpassed in range and intensity anything we have previously witnessed. They were concerned with the education of children and of adults, and with the content of education; they placed enormous emphasis on the rational power of knowledge and truth, and on social contact; they lectured, debated, published and organised; they looked to education and to their own educational efforts to transform society.

The National Union of the Working Classes

A new working-class political radicalism was also being generated, particularly in the early 1830s, with an educational content and impact which continued the older style and tradition. Its main vehicle was the National Union of the Working Classes, formed in 1831, with the dual purpose of trade union protection and a campaign for parliamentary reform: meetings were sometimes described as being of 'delegates of trades, and others' (Wallas, 1898, 271; *Poor Man's Guardian*, unnumbered (24 June), 1831, 6). The focus of the new organisation, which had roots in the Owenite British Association for promoting Co-operative Knowledge, became the fight for a free press, against the 'taxes on knowledge'. Just as women were involved in many Owenite activities, so were they also active in the NUWC, including a related 'Female Society' called Friends of the Oppressed, directed particularly to assisting 'the wives and families of those suffering under oppression' (*Poor Man's Guardian*, no. 65, 1832, 528). The NUWC spearheaded the working-class campaign for the 1832 reform bill, as the National Political Union did for the radical middle class. It continued its agitation after the Whigs had in 1832 'betrayed the people ... frustrating the hopes their own promises had evoked' (Linton, 1879, 53). A 'declaration of the rights of man' issued by the NUWC in 1831 was directed towards the acquisition of rights and liberties, freedom of expression and the press, equal legal rights and parliamentary representation—and education:

> Instruction is the want of all; society and government ought, therefore, to do all in their power, to favour the progress of reason and truth; and to place instruction within the reach of all.

The means at the disposal of the NUWC were organisation (into branches and district divisions), meetings, the press and publications, and 'the active talent, zeal, and industry of the representatives of the Union'. The committee directed, in order to produce 'a real Union, and not a mere chaos', that class leaders should be appointed for each district, that there should be an average of twenty-five members per class, that class leaders should collect names and addresses and monthly subscriptions, and that class leaders together should constitute a committee (Rowe, 1970, 29, 32, 50).

The organisation became solidly established on this structure of class meetings (often explicitly compared to that of the Methodist church). Discussion often centred on the writings of Paine, Godwin and Owen, and the 'unstamped' press was circulated and discussed. The weekly meetings were 'for political instruction, by readings and discussions' (Linton, 1879, 41). A new momentum of reform organisation was established throughout the country, and many of the new organisations followed the model of the NUWC (Wearmouth, 1937, 90-9; Wearmouth, 1948, 66-84). The classes were a mechanism of political education, aimed at helping to secure primarily political rights and a free press. The political radicals found themselves having to conduct a dialogue with the Owenites—and many of the members of the NUWC indeed combined support for Owenite co-operation with a commitment to political reform. In the autumn of 1832, the *Poor Man's Guardian* (virtually the organ of the NUWC) reported joint meetings with Owen and his followers, aimed at finding ways to unity. 'The disciples of Mr. Owen', said the *Guardian*, 'may differ from us as to the means ... but they have precisely the same eventual object in view, namely, to establish for the workman dominion over the fruits of his own industry' :

> Let us all unite against the common enemy, and turn against him his own weapons. Above all, let the Radical take the Owenite by the hand, and the Owenite do the same by the Radical, for both parties are the real, and only real friends of the working people (*Poor Man's Guardian*, no. 67, 1832, 538).

The appeal apparently went unheeded, and Owen continued to be contemptuous of what he saw as the misguided efforts of the political radicals. Education was discussed in the NUWC, though not as extensively or with such a wide frame of reference as in Owenite organisations. One indication of the specific political context of the discussion is given by a resolution adopted by a Birmingham 'public meeting of the working classes and others' in August 1831, in support of the 'free circulation of knowledge'. In attacking the taxes on knowledge the meeting expressed its 'regret, not unmixed with indignation', at the government grant of 'an enormous annuity for educating a princess ... whilst it postpones the consideration of a question on the result of which must mainly depend the confirmed ignorance or knowledge of a whole people'. The mover of this resolution is reported to have

> regretted to find so much aristocracy prevalent throughout society. This he attributed in a great degree to the poorer classes being 'educated' as it was called by the rich or their underlings—that is, they were taught just as much as would suit the purposes of the latter.

This was true both of the National school and of the mechanics' institute. He 'strongly urged the working classes to take their education into their hands' (*Poor Man's Guardian*, no. 7, 1831, 52, 56). J. A. Roebuck, radical leader of the education movement in the reformed Parliament, addressed the NUWC on the subject of education in 1834 (Leader, 1897, 61). The organisation was abandoned the following year.

Working-class and popular radicalism was, as we have seen, not homogeneous. There were movements and activities associated with Owen, Henry Hunt, Sir Francis Burdett, Carlile and others, and differences of emphasis even within organisations. A police informer reported on these organisations that

> the whole of the leaders of these and many of the
> followers are in opposition to each other and are all
> disagreeing as to their ways of thinking and obtaining
> redress, but the whole of which have begun to be more
> anxious to be known and continue to do so since the
> French Revolution and have had a good many extra
> followers (Wiener, 1969, 238).

Although there were such divergences, the working-class radical movement did indeed now have 'extra followers', and the various parts of the movement had enough in common to strengthen the sense of working-class radical purpose. Some of the later Chartist leaders drew their energies from a whole range of these activities in the early 1830s: G. J. Harney was in these years 'imbibing from the contents of the radical unstamped a belief in political democracy ... a belief which he had also heard from the speakers of the National Union of the Working Classes. The social doctrines which he read were generally Owenite in their tone' (Schoyen, 1958, 8). The most unifying of all activities in this period was the fight for the unstamped press.

Radical publishing

Radical publishers and editors saw the role of the press as a liberating and educational one. Oppression could not stand up to the power of truth. From the time of the Six Acts of 1819 the radical press had been labouring under the burden of the stamp tax and legal restrictions on 'blasphemous and seditious' publications. The question of knowledge and publications was therefore given a central place in the activities of the new reformers. The defiant, illegal, unstamped press had a sense of the power of the written word. It also recognised its role as the mouthpiece of movements: the unstamped, it has been said, 'kept the NUWC transparent' (Hollis, 1970, 268).

As in the period of Cobbett's *Register* the popular radical press penetrated far and was sought by radical working men as in itself the embodiment of a political and social ideal. At the height of the campaign against the stamp tax, in 1834-5,

> something like 150,000 copies of the unstamped papers were defiantly distributed each week; every copy likely to be passed from hand to hand, studied in coffee-houses and taverns, and read aloud to groups of non-readers.... Even journeyman handloom silk weavers of Spitalfields and Bethnal Green, desperately poor though they were, tried hard to save a copper to buy a copy (Plummer, 1971, 49).

In 1832 there were complaints that on Saturdays people in the market place in Leicester sold 'all sorts of papers, some ... quite profligate and blasphemous, calculated to set the lower orders against all that is decent and orderly in the land' (Patterson, 1954, 290). In this kind of public defiance lay the political strength of the movement; the unstamped press could be seen to be speaking out, by its very presence, on behalf of working-class radicalism.

Self-educated working men

The publishers who, in the tradition of Carlile, also provided the movement with its books and pamphlets played the same role. Press, publications, organisation, agitation, discussion—all merged in a widespread combination of working-class political and cultural experience. An important feature of this experience was its relationship to the literacy acquired by many working-class children through the formal means of schooling. On the basis of attendance at either a Sunday school or a National or British school many working men had obtained the tools with which to fashion this experience. At the same school, at home, in apprenticeship, others found the basic means of self-education. Critical though radicals often were of education 'from above', in a church or middle-class mould, others were only too glad of the basic education they had found. In Sheffield the Lancasterian school was remembered with gratitude by radical Isaac Ironside, and in 1825 he sent a contribution of 2/6d. to it, 'trusting that the school may still be a public blessing' (Salt, 1971, 186). Many radicals began their careers, like Detrosier for example, on the basis of a Sunday school education. Of the period of the Hampden Clubs Bamford explains that 'the Sunday schools of the preceding thirty years had produced many working men of sufficient talent to become readers, writers and speakers in the village meetings for parliamentary reform' (Bamford, 1893, I, 12).

The self-taught tradition of an earlier period was therefore continued, very often from the narrow base provided by some form of schooling. Throughout the first half of the century this tradition fed on every means available for obtaining the first steps in education. A. E. Dobbs quotes a vivid example from the field of night schools (which were often created in association with Sunday schools and by many radical organisations). Night schools

became scenes of considerable energy, and helped to satisfy the desire for self-improvement inspired by certain aspects of the Industrial Revolution. At a candle factory in Vauxhall, in the year 1847, some dozen boys set an example by starting a night class on their own initiative, 'hiding ... behind a bench two or three times a week, after they had done their work and had their tea, to practise writing on scraps of paper with worn-out pens begged from the counting house' (Dobbs, 1919, 156, quoting the *Quarterly Review*).

It is not easy to judge what the responses of literate working men were in general to any early education they had received, since few testimonies remain. A proportion, however, must have shared the view of Thomas Cooper, the best known of the self-educated radicals, who described his narrow experience at the local monitorial school, but made the point that 'our frequent practice in spelling, and the working over and over, of the four introductory rules of arithmetic, formed at least a good preparation for larger acquirements' (Cooper, 1879, 13).

So proud, in fact, were working men of their self-acquired accomplishments, that there was sometimes in working-class organisations an uncritical acceptance of the low level of attainment in the schools, and in fact an interpretation of it as a virtue. This attitude is illustrated in a story told by Timothy Claxton, son of a day labourer, in a book he published in 1844, advising mechanics on self-education and mutual instruction. Claxton described with admiration an incident involving Edmund Stone, the mathematician who was son of a gardener to the Duke of Argyle. The Duke found a copy of Newton's *Principia* on the grass, and discovered to his surprise that it belonged to the gardener's seventeen-year-old son. The boy explained to the Duke that a servant had taught him to read, and asked rhetorically: 'Does any one need to know any more than the letters to learn everything else that he wishes?'

(Claxton, 1844, 6-7). Hence, on the part of many—though by no means all—working men, the feeling that it was enough for schools to teach working-class children their letters: the rest was best acquired independently. Working-class radical resistance to middle-class philanthropy, and even to middle-class radicalism, led not only to an independent movement (including for education) but also to independent casts of mind, which saw Sunday and monitorial schools as useful preliminaries to what Cooper called 'larger acquirements'.

Education and popular radicalism

It was from such starting points that the various forms of mutual improvement among working men continued to operate. Efforts at self-improvement were the story of 'the unrecorded, the unremembered, the undiscoverable'. They were embodied primarily in 'the small "mutual improvement society"', without name or habitation, which kept together but for a few years' (Ludlow and Jones, 1867, 24). Groups of working men might meet in William Lovett's coffee-house for political discussion and call themselves 'social reformers' (Lovett, 1876, 89), or they might meet in one another's homes, club together to buy books or stationery, or meet for discussion and mutual encouragement wherever it was possible. In 1836 Francis Place wrote to 'Mr Morton, Journeyman Carpenter' to say that he had been told 'of your intention to form societies in various places to consist of working men for the purpose of mutual instruction'. Place offered a lot of detailed advice, much of it based on his own experience of the London Corresponding Society (Rowe, 1970, 156-8). The informal, impermanent organisation of men dedicated to study, discussion and mutual help was a feature of the 1830s, just as it had been of the 1810s and would be of the 1850s. From the 1810s there had also developed an adult school movement, at which some 30,000 men were estimated to have learned to read by 1849 (Yeaxlee, 1925, I, 199-209). Working men attended classes run by Owenites together with the children. In Northumberland and Durham 'grown men were to be found sitting next to children in school-class' (Challinor and Ripley, 1968, 53). In countless ways men found education, educated themselves, educated one another. Radical politics were never far away from some form of adult education.

As in the case of the 1790s it is no sense to diminish the importance and impact of working-class radicalism to identify it closely with education. Educational, social and political advance were all components of the ideals and the action which became part of working-class consciousness. The process has been described in terms of levels of idealism:

> the lower idealism of the trade unions and Chartism on the one hand, and the higher idealism of Owenism and Associationism on the other, could not be fused in a political programme, but they were brought together through social and educational ventures. In this process adult education was significant (Harrison, 1961, 91).

Education and the press were in this sense the main unifying forces of radical movements. The essential contribution of Owen to all of these movements was the sense of the vulnerability of the human character to the power of environment, what he and countless others after him called 'circumstances'. He, and the image of New Lanark, contributed enormously to confidence in the possibility of changing both circumstances and character. The radical press and reformers of all kinds went on using the Owenite analysis, and adopting the enthusiasm for enlightenment to which Owen had given added vigour. They argued generally, like the *Co-operator* in 1828, that the working class were acquiring and must increasingly acquire knowledge: 'no man ever lost the love of knowledge when once acquired, neither will the working classes undervalue that which will assuredly lead them to independence' (*Co-operator*, no. 8, 1828, 3). Like Detrosier they believed that working-class unity plus knowledge would change the face of society: 'what are the means by which joy may be restored to the scathed heart, comfort to the cheerless home, independence and happiness to honourable industry? Union and knowledge' (Detrosier, 1831, 1). Like the early Chartists they believed in education 'not as a charity, but as a right, a right derivable from society itself' (Lovett, 1876, I, 142).

Emphases were different, and in the 1830s some militant radicals saw educational demands as a distraction from the prime, political demands. But a preoccupation with education was constant in the radical literature of the early 1830s. The ideals of which it formed an integral part in turn sustained the energies of a class still seeking to extricate itself from the worst effects of the Industrial Revolution. Ideals were explicit, and the impact of the striving after them was direct. Schools had an impact as much in what working men made of them as in what their organisers intended to achieve. Charles Knight, as we have seen, was one of the commentators who saw elementary education and popular literature as 'efficient instruments of amelioration' in the social conditions of the people. What the movements of the 1820s and early 1830s demonstrate, however, is that the working class were not only 'ameliorated' from outside, but also contributed substantially to their own self-identification, their own self-improvement, their own independent vision of progress. Patricia Hollis has emphasised that education was in this period a political battle

> fought out in a dozen and one sectors of the educational world. The arguments for and against the taxes on knowledge were carried over from one sphere of popular education to the next, from mechanics institutes to national schools, from cheap newspapers to the hours the British Museum stayed open, from the availability of factory schools to the desirability of public libraries' (Hollis, 1970, 8-9).

Education was closely allied to questions of rights and freedoms of all kinds. The movements which advocated education were in themselves an education.

The essential impact of these movements was in the strengthening of working-class ideals, in further elevating working men 'in their own opinion'. Henry Hetherington, radical publisher-in-chief of the 1830s, told a meeting of the NUWC in 1832 of 'the importance of the *Poor Man's Guardian*, and the power of a free press'. His *Guardian* had had 'an extraordinary effect upon the daily papers, who did not now call them "mob" and "rabble", and "swinish multitude", but they were all at once become "operatives" and "working men"' (*Poor Man's Guardian*, no. 69, 1832, 556). The comment, and the laughter with which it was received, are indicative of the new level of confidence.

5

Chartism

Working Men's Associations

The London Working Men's Association, which heralded
what was soon to become the Chartist movement, was
born in 1836. The first intention of its creators was to fight
for a cheap press, but both the London Association and
others modelled on it absorbed this and other objectives
into a wider programme of political reform. An outstanding feature of the London WMA was the detailed educational programme to which it committed itself. The initial
objectives of the Association were not, indeed, concerned
with parliamentary reform. It proposed, as we have seen,
to 'draw into one bond of unity the intelligent and influential portion of the working classes'. It proposed to fight
for the removal of laws 'that prevent the free circulation
of thought through the medium of a cheap and honest
press', and to promote 'the education of the rising generation'. It proposed to collect information and statistics on
labour conditions, hold meetings and publish material with
a view to improving the workers' conditions, and 'to form
a library of reference and useful information' where members could 'associate for mental improvement' (Howell,
1972, 36-9).

Similar associations were created elsewhere. Henry Hetherington attended the inaugural meeting of the Sheffield Working Men's Association in October 1837, founded amid a 'new spirit of revolt' (Salt, 1971, 190). An organisation established in Leicester in 1836 linked up with the London Association two years later as a result of a visit by Hetherington (Patterson, 1954, 296-7). The London Association had, in fact, appointed members to act as 'missionaries'. Howell's history of the London Association indicates associated organisations in 1837 at Bath, Hull, Leeds, Halifax and elsewhere; by the end of 1838 there were eighty-one Working Men's Associations and thirty radical or other associations in friendly correspondence with the London Association (Howell, 1972, 84-5, 89). From whatever starting points they came, they began to formulate afresh wide programmes of political reform, and became one of the important constituent parts of Chartism.

The London Association issued an address on education in 1837 which is an important document in the history of educational ideas and campaigns. Its philosophy is outlined in a passage which stresses (with an emphasis new in radical working-class literature) the need for government provision of a system of education for all classes:

> poverty, inequality, and political injustice, are involved in giving to one portion of society the blessings of education, and leaving the other in ignorance ... the working classes, who are in general the victims of this system of oppression and ignorance, have just cause of complaint against all partial systems of education.

It protested against the 'modicum of mental light' that the wealthy had so far permitted, or failed to prevent, and it argued for education as a basic right. It put forward a detailed plan for locally administered education, under elected 'school committees', administering national and rate-provided funds. It proposed the erection of infant schools, preparatory schools (for children aged six to nine), high schools (nine to twelve), and colleges. Buildings were to be open in the evenings for adult education. This programme, shaped very largely by William Lovett, was later to be the basis of *Chartism*, a pamphlet in which Lovett and John Collins put forward the most far-reaching programme of education to emerge out of the Chartist movement. The London WMA, in this programme, as well as in a new dimension of interest in international issues, and in its detailed concern with political rights and universal male suffrage (Lovett's original inclusion of female suffrage was overruled), represents a new departure in its total concern, embodied in programmes which rested on foundations prepared by several generations of popular and working-class radical endeavour.

Other contributory factors must not be forgotten, if the dimensions of Chartism are to be properly understood. The new Poor Law was, after 1834, as much a focus (and often more so) of popular discontent as questions of political reform—especially in the industrial districts. Questions of the reduction of working hours, the protection of factory children, freedom of the press, trade-union and co-operative organisation and the Corn Laws, played vital parts at different times and places in shaping the mass agitation subsumed under the name of Chartism. Social realities were always present behind the political demands of the Charter. Educational ideals were not jettisoned in the search for political justice. It was not only the Sheffield Working Men's Association whose aim was 'to raise ourselves in everything good and great' (Salt, 1971, 191).

Chartism and educational ideals

Out of the activities of the London WMA came the People's Charter in 1837. It was embodied in a petition which contained the principles of universal suffrage, equal representation, annual parliaments, no property qualification, vote by ballot, and payment of members. The Charter was intended to 'form a rallying-point for radical reformers' (Lovett, 1876, I, 120-1). For a decade the Charter was, indeed, such a rallying point—with peaks of Chartist activity in 1838, 1842 and 1848. It brought together reformers of many kinds, with an overriding commitment to the new programme, and grounded in working-class radicalism. With changes in motives for action, in economic conditions and in local conditions and preoccupations, the nature of the movement itself changed. Chartist 'physical force' and 'moral force' wings were identified, but the distinction was often flimsy, and it was easy for many, with the turn of a tide, to move into the one, or both, or neither. Only until 1839 was there a real measure of unity, an interlocking of opinion at national level. The uncertainties of the Chartist Convention in London and Birmingham, the first arrests, the failure of the first Chartist petition, and divided opinions about the future conduct of the movement, led to its deepening fragmentation and the establishment of sectional hostilities and vocabularies. By 1842 fragmentation at leadership level was deep, but although from then onwards it was not a united movement it was capable of acting in unity. Its demonstrations were a vast coming together of popular grievances and ideals. Thomas Attwood, the banker who led the Birmingham Political Union, an important force in the creation of Chartism, told a Scottish audience in 1838 that such 'great meetings ... enable the people, by the peaceful but overwhelming expression of public opinion, to command those great and necessary changes in society which, without them, would only be effected by years of anarchy and blood' (Wakefield, 1885, 327).

What Chartism did was make what Carlyle called 'the condition-of-England-question' a central feature of political life. It brought together many of the traditions and commitments that we have discussed into, at times, a single-minded thrust towards political and social change. It recruited the efforts of diverse movements which had shaped working-class consciousness and confidence. Chartism provided a basis for a closer combination of political, social, educational and cultural objectives. Chartist opinion was profoundly concerned with education in the broad sense that we have encountered in previous movements; Chartists were profoundly engaged in educational activities.

Even when the Charter had been launched, and in the midst of intense political activity, as one historian of the movement records, 'the educational side was not forgotten':

It was continually kept in mind by the little group of London agitators and taken up with enthusiasm in many sections. The *Weekly Advertiser* pledges itself to 'advocate the establishment of a national system of education on purely secular grounds'. *The Reformer* says that 'Popular education will occupy a large share of our attention', while the *Chartist Circular* strongly urges upon the Scots Chartists the advisability of forming schools (Faulkner, 1916, 49).

The Chartist press advocated and provided intellectual enlightenment, and Chartist principles were discussed in the movement in relation to the whole gamut of social and cultural experience—from teetotalism to Christianity, from libraries to currency. Although there were strongly based Christian Chartist movements and Chartist churches (in Scotland and Birmingham chiefly), the underlying tenor of Chartist educational opinion was secular. Chartist experience 'swelled both the demand and the necessity of popular education' (Hovell, 1918, 311), as well as intensifying individual efforts at self-education and collective attempts at mutual improvement and the provision of educational facilities by popular movements themselves.

Lovett and Collins

It is in this context, as well as that of rival 'moral force' and 'physical force' ideologies within the movement, that the most explicit Chartist educational programme—that of Lovett and Collins—has to be seen. It is misleading to describe Chartism in terms of stable 'wings', or to define this programme entirely under Feargus O'Connor's contemptuous label of 'knowledge Chartism'. Lovett and Collins's *Chartism*, written in gaol and published in 1840, was a programme, like all Chartist programmes, for 'securing to all men their equal political and social rights'. By 1840 there were divergent views about how to achieve them, but *Chartism* was as much in the mainstream of radical opinion as its critics. It was not a programme for education in the abstract; it was a rejection of 'exclusive' schemes of education, and offered a specifically Chartist scheme for the education of all. The National Association it proposed was intended to work for the principles of the People's Charter, and to launch a nation-wide scheme of education in the hands of the people. It proposed the erection of schools (infant, preparatory, high, agricultural, industrial) and 'normal schools' for teacher training, the arrangement of evening lectures, discussions and entertainment, libraries and publications. It proposed detailed rules for the administration of the system, school plans and rules; it discussed what we would today call the psychology and sociology of education, and the importance of education for what in the twentieth century has been called 'citizenship'. It discussed in detail desirable curriculum and teaching arrangements for the different types of school, and compared different approaches to curriculum content and teaching methods, and even offered specimen lesson cards. It was in every sense, in the words of the programme's sub-title, 'a new organisation of the people'. It was a study in popular democracy, discussing the election of local boards to control the schools, the election of school 'superintendents', the selection of teachers, and committee and financial procedure. The whole, financed by popular subscription, was to be a vast exercise in political and cultural progress (Lovett and Collins, 1840, *passim*). It rejected the monitorial system by emphasising the supreme importance of teachers adequate in number and training. Each teacher training college was to have a library, museum, laboratory, sitting rooms and sleeping rooms. The people must not neglect the important duty of 'rewarding and honouring the teachers of their children', so as to develop the science of education and secure the services of 'men of genius and intelligence' (*ibid.*, 76-7). The authors refer to most of the important contemporary educationists.

Lovett came out of prison in 1840 ' "almost crazy" with the belief that the Chartists ought to apply all their funds to building great schools, where the children would receive a thorough literary, technical, and sociological education' (Wallas, 1898, 378). O'Connor and the *Northern Star* were furious at the whole scheme, the latter describing it in

1841 as 'nothing more or less than a new mode of canvassing support for Mechanics' Institutes and the Brougham system of making one portion of the working class disgusted with all below them'. People who worked sixteen hours a day and were then thrown into workhouses 'as unfit for use, have very little relish for any protracted course of study or "education", though it were certain in one hundred and twenty years to gain the Charter for them' (Jones, 1938, 128-9). The scheme had support in some radical and Chartist circles, though the direct impact of the book was probably not great. In the 1850s Robert Lowery, ex-Chartist and Liberal, described *Chartism* as 'one of the most comprehensive and practical plans for elevating the working men which has yet been offered to the public' (Harrison and Hollis, 1967, 509). Francis Place, ultra-cautious as always, told Lovett that his programme was 'rank sectarianism. . . . It would be a Chartist Popedom' (*ibid.*, 117).

On the 'left' of Chartism there were inevitably ambiguous views about education, and a disdain of attempts such as Lovett's to put education at the forefront of Chartist priorities. From the late 1830s 'educationism', together with Owenism and other social panaceas, were seen by O'Connor, O'Brien and others as distractions from the central political purpose of Chartism. R. G. Gammage, bitter about the wrecking role he believed O'Connor to have played in the movement, considered how happy it would have been if Lovett's plan

had met with general adoption, always taking care that it was never perverted to mere middle class purposes. We might then in a few years have seen a popular power built up, of sufficient strength to have withstood all the blasts of the enemies of Democracy. But this was the very last thing that O'Connor desired. He never sought to raise the Chartist body by enlightening its members.... The building of halls and schools, and the establishment of circulating libraries, would not only have led to the better instruction of the people, but it would have given them a material interest, not only in joining, but in sustaining the movement, which would then have been something better than a record of absurdities, disasters, and defeats (Gammage, 1854, 196-197).

Allowances for internal frictions within the movement must be made in considering responses to Lovett or to O'Connor, but the essential problem was undoubtedly one of priorities. O'Connor and his supporters and the *Northern Star* were not against education : they regarded political action as primary. The *Northern Star* returned repeatedly to the theme that, as it wrote in 1846, 'the political enfranchisement of the whole male adult population, is an indispensable preliminary to every kind of educational, social and physical improvement' (Simon, 1960, 271). With the highly articulated political programme and campaigns of the Chartist movement had come a conflict in interpreting the relationship between politics and education. The situation was different from what it had been in the 1790s or even in the 1820s. The working class had now established independent forms of action, identified its own ideals, achieved a considerable level of organisation, seen —in and around 1832—the inadequacies of alliance with middle-class reformers, and had enough experience of overarching theories and programmes to be able to focus also on specific objectives. In a period of immense enthusiasm, high hopes and repeated disappointments it was inevitable that working-class attitudes to education should contain greater ambiguities.

Education remained an item of Chartist debate and programmes to the end. One of the resolutions that Thomas Cooper intended to move at the 1846 Chartist convention (at which he had a confrontation with O'Connor and was then excluded) proclaimed a 'conviction of the paramount value of education, tolerance of the opinions of others, and morality of life, as constituents in Chartist character' (Gammage, 1854, 275). Five years later, in 1851, a Chartist convention adopted a programme which proclaimed that 'as every man has a right to the means of physical life, so he has to the means of mental activity.... Education should, therefore, be national, universal, gratuitous and, to a certain extent, compulsory.' It recommended free, state-supported schools, colleges and universities, compulsory education 'in the common branches of learning', optional higher education, and industrial schools which would supersede apprenticeship (Saville, 1952, 260). What is even more evident than the education debate, however, is the scale of Chartist educational activity.

Chartist classes, schools and halls

In his study of the class meeting tradition Wearmouth underlines the extent of Chartist educational organisation of this kind. By the end of 1839 political classes had been organised widely in the Midlands and the North, with ten to twenty members in each class, and with purposes and activities similar to those we have seen in earlier radical movements. Sunderland Chartists were urged to enrol in classes and make them 'an important medium for the diffusion of intelligence'. Classes were reported in 1840 from London to Middlesborough, from Liverpool to Brighton, from Plymouth to Durham. Female Chartist classes were formed, for example in Oldham, and teetotal Chartist classes existed in Dewsbury and elsewhere. Such classes, as before, were a combination of political activity and adult education. The Durham Political Union in 1840 recommended that class members should read 'works of history, and especially the history of our own country, discussing its great events philosophically, not as mere matters of fact, but noting their bearing on our present state'. Newcastle-upon-Tyne working men were urged to join classes, and to 'let each class constitute itself a fireside republic' (Wearmouth, 1948, 126-43).

The classes were part of a wider spectrum of educational activities, which in Leicester, for instance, 'included lectures, reading rooms, discussions, schools, papers and pamphlets' (Greenwood, 1973, 148). Chartist halls were opened in many places to provide independent premises for political and educational activities, one of the first being completed in Manchester in 1840. In the 1840s they appeared in towns large and small, different in scale, financed by collection, subscription and loan, sometimes purpose-built, sometimes using chapel or inn. They provided a place where regular lectures could be given and visiting speakers could be heard, often because town halls or other premises were refused to the Chartists for meetings. They frequently housed libraries and reading rooms (Simon, 1960, 243-7). They were often explicitly hostile to the middle-class patronage of the mechanics' institutes.

Chartist schools of one kind or another were associated with many of the halls and other focal points of Chartist activity, though the extent of the provision of schools by Chartists is far from clear. Examples of known Chartist schools include one run in a chapel in Nottingham, schools for children and young men run by the Chartist church in Birmingham, and day and Sunday schools at Carpenters'

Hall (Manchester), Elland, Birmingham, Leicester, Oldham and elsewhere (*ibid.*, 251-3; Jones, 1938, 156; Hovell, 1918, 200). The Chartist services and churches which were organised in Scotland in the 1840s gave rise to a variety of educational activities, including classes and schools for the children of Chartists. Chartist schools of this kind were set up at Leven, Aberdeen, Arbroath, Perth, Hamilton and elsewhere. Many had over a hundred pupils, and one at Greenock had 300 (Wilson, 1970, 149; Wright, 1953, 101-3). Linked with the Chartist churches were also mutual improvement societies, evening classes, dramatic and other activities. The Chartist schools, comments Leslie Wright, were 'a bold experiment in positive Radicalism' (*ibid.*, 102-3).

It is as a sustained exercise in adult education in its broadest sense that Chartism is most important in the history of education. Thomas Cooper, the most famous of the Chartist educators, organised an adult Sunday school in 1841 in Leicester which may have been unique in one sense, but is indicative of the kind of educational energies which suffused the movement. He used the Old and New Testaments as class books, together with Channing's *Self-Culture* and other tracts. The classes were named after Andrew Marvell, John Hampden, Major Cartwright, Milton, Washington, Cobbett and others. They sang, wrote and published Chartist hymns. Cooper 'recited the history of England, and set the portraits of great Englishmen before young Chartists'. He took up and taught geology and phrenology, 'and made the young men acquainted, elementally, with the knowledge of the time' (Cooper, 1879, 41, 46-7, 164-72). Other such Sunday schools appeared in Leicester, and were reflected in similar efforts elsewhere—albeit not always on such an ambitious basis. At their simplest such efforts were simply a continued form of the mutual improvement which was now a traditional feature of working-class educational activity. W. J. Linton, radical engraver, living at Woodford, 'busied himself with opposing the church rate and forming a Mutual Instruction Society for the working men of Walthamstow'. His mutual instruction work began in connection with Chartism, when he convened a meeting to hear two missionaries from the Chartist Convention of 1839. Those who attended were ostracised locally and could not obtain a room for the second meeting, 'so, on a wintry day in early 1840, Linton gathered them in a clearing in Epping Forest and addressed them from a tree-stump upon the right of public discussion and the high morality of their aims' (Smith, 1973, 43-4). This was mutual improvement in the sense both of organised political activity and of the more informal working-class efforts at self-education.

The impact of Chartism

The total cultural impact of Chartism cannot be underestimated. Chartist politics were an intensely educational and cultural force. Working-class Chartists wrote hymns and poems, lectured and listened to itinerant lectures like Henry Vincent and Robert Lowery. Through Chartism they developed an interest in literature, history, science, and the whole range of what Cooper called 'the knowledge of the time'. Harriet Martineau wrote of radical working men in this period that they 'spent their hard earnings, their spare hours, their sleeping hours, their health, their repose, to promote the education the state did not give. By wonderful efforts, they established schools, institutes, lecture and reading rooms, and circulated knowledge among their class in every way they could think of' (Martineau, 1877, 263). There is a direct relationship between the political and social programme and activities of Chartism, on the one hand, and the effects of the working man to educate himself and his fellows on the other.

As with earlier radical movements it is also important to stress the vital political and cultural contribution of the Chartist press. It played a central role in helping working people to define their own political and cultural positions. Dorothy Thompson underlines the related facts that Chartist propaganda often 'took the form of argument, a dialogue with the middle classes', and that in spite of often low levels of literacy among working people 'written and printed material was an essential part of the lives of them all' (Thompson, 1971, 13). The *Northern Star* was of outstanding importance in this respect. Begun as a radical newspaper in 1837, it adopted the Chartist programme and became the mouthpiece of the movement in the north of England (Glasgow, 1954, 66). It was described in 1840, as we have seen, as 'a bond of union':

> The *Northern Star* is only the consequence of an advance made by the unenfranchised in combination and power. The Black Dwarfs of the earlier part of this century were an emanation from London alone; the country readers were disciples, not co-operatives.... The *Northern Star* is a bond of union, and an organ of a numerous and influential party among the unenfranchised, diffused throughout the whole nation (*Tait's Edinburgh Magazine*, vol. VII, 1840, 811).

Chartism itself was a combination of varied regional as well as national preoccupations; the Chartist press was both a national and a regional phenomenon. The *Northern Star* was a bond of union in the North because it was of the North. Local propaganda—including the radical press—helped further to break the sense of 'disciplehood' and to encourage more active, local responses to political and economic situations. It encouraged a more positive radical culture.

Chartism is a global description of a movement which spanned two decades of organisation and activity. It describes a movement which was variegated within itself, and which also had a variety of relationships to bodies of opinion which have become identified with other labels—including the factory movement, the ten-hour movement, Tory radicalism, and the fight against the new Poor Law. Within Chartism and in association with it were groups with a dominant interest in temperance or Christianity, currency or land reform. In some places Chartists probably contributed to building Owenite Halls of Science, and met on Owenite premises. The dialogues between political radicals and Owenites that took place in the early 1830s were not unknown in the Chartist period, and included at least one attempt to bring members of both movements into a united social-democratic partnership, with political objectives (Schoyen, 1958, 184). The trade unionist, the ten-hour man, the educational or any kind of reformer, did not have to lose his other identity in Chartism. Chartism was, in fact, the first of the popular and working-class radical movements which absorbed, sustained and often gave added impetus to movements which were otherwise isolated and weak.

Lovett and the other early Chartist leaders intended the People's Charter to be a rallying point for popular radicalism, and this is what it became. The working-class radicalism of the 1830s and 1840s marked profound changes in scale and social impact. The political dimensions of Chartism are best summarised in terms of what has been called 'Chartism-democracy', or the issue of 'the political recognition of the working classes. The Chartists had brought the possibility of democracy down from the realm of speculation and high constitutional debate into the hot arena of mass agitation' (Gillespie, 1927, 5). The impact of Chartism was felt through forms of mass action and organisation, and national recognition of the existence not only of mass agitation, but also of the social and political realities which it signalled. The range of the Chartists' commitments was summarised by an old Chartist in the 1880s:

they took a leading part in agitating in favour of the ten hours question, the repeal of the taxes on knowledge, education, co-operation, civil and religious liberty and the land question, for they were the true pioneers in all the great movements of their time (Wilson, 1887, 13-14).

In educational terms the responses across this period were basically twofold. In the presence of political upheaval, and with a third or so of the male population still illiterate, the search continued among middle-class radicals and philanthropists for ways of developing the school system. Parliamentary grants were increased, a committee of the Privy Council was formed to supervise its distribution and the inspection of elementary schools, the pupil teacher system was inaugurated and attempts were made to extend national action through legislation, on the education of factory and other children. Educators and legislators engaged in this process were conscious of the dangers of illiteracy and mass agitation, and in some cases their plans were designed precisely to avert these dangers.

The second response was that of the working-class movements themselves. Chartism made its educational impact in the forms that we have discussed, and perhaps most of all in the direct incentive it gave to working men to develop the skills of communication and to play an active political and cultural role. In the classes and the movement at large 'many Chartists learned to read, discuss, speak, debate, instruct: they grew wise and skilled in "promulgating truth"' (Wearmouth, 1948, 142). In the Chartist press many working men found 'their sole text-book of history, political geography, English literature, economics and political theory' (Slosson, 1916, 199). The Chartist movement was widely concerned about and engaged in processes of education at all levels. It was itself an educational process in the radical tradition of the previous half-century.

6

Middle-class radicalism, 1835-1848

The radical voice in the 1830s

By the second half of the 1830s the middle-class radicals
had representation in the reformed Parliament, were having
to respond to strong popular demands for wider parliamentary representation and for social reforms, and were
beginning to organise more effectively as an educational
pressure group. Nonconformist and radical attacks were
continuing against the universities of Oxford and
Cambridge, and against the traditional curricula and
objectives of the public and endowed schools. The most
rapid current of change in the ancient universities was not
to occur, however, until the appointment of commissions
of inquiry in 1850, and the current of change was also
not to run strong in the old endowed schools until well
into the second half of the century. In the late 1830s and
1840s the focus of middle-class radical opinion was
essentially on local and parliamentary efforts to secure a
national system of popular education.

For many of the middle-class reformers educational
progress was a necessary preliminary to any expansion of
political democracy, and the reformed Parliament was
repeatedly faced with demands for legislation. Some

radical MPs opposed the 1833 parliamentary grant as an inadequate step, and throughout the 1830s and 1840s education remained a serious parliamentary issue. Brougham was by now in the Lords, and the educational issue was pressed in the House of Commons by a new generation of radicals—J. A. Roebuck, Joseph Hume and others. Roebuck told Parliament in 1833 that in the next session he would 'devise a means for the universal and national education of the whole' people. When Lord John Russell, in response, moved that £20,000 be voted for the purposes of education, Hume said he would oppose the vote as being 'too small for any national purpose' (Buckmaster, 1862, 5). Roebuck and his colleagues in the Commons, and Brougham in the Lords, made attempts in the following years to promote inquiries and extend parliamentary action.

Thomas Wyse and the Central Society

One of the strongest links between parliamentary efforts by radical MPs and a new educational movement being inaugurated in the country was the activity of Thomas Wyse, radical Irish MP and chairman of the Central Society of Education. Wyse had also played a major part in the late 1820s and early 1830s in the establishment of a system of education in Ireland which was an important spur to the English radicals in this period. The events which led, in 1831, to the creation of a board of education to superintend a national system of Irish elementary education demonstrated the possibility of overcoming sectarian differences. The schools established by the new board were to provide common education for all children, with time set aside on one or two days in the week for religious instruction. Catholics, Anglicans and dissenters sat on the board (Akensen, 1970, 107-22). This fact, together with the common secular education over which they presided, served as stimuli to the English radicals in the early 1830s in their attempts to secure a national system of education. The important role that Thomas Wyse had played in bringing about the Irish solution lent even more weight to his efforts and to those of the Central Society. This Society was a new type of organisation, designed to collect and disseminate information, to exert pressure, to influence local action and national legislation. Created in London in 1837, the society sought to 'arouse the mass of the nation from its apathy upon the important subject which it has undertaken to advocate' (Central Society, 1837, 26). Statistical societies were beginning to collect serious information about school places and attendance, and related social problems such as housing and employment. Wyse summarised the Manchester data in the first publication of the Central Society:

> The Reports of the Statistical Society of Manchester present a painful and humiliating picture of the general mass of our so named, but misnamed, education.... Bad sites, bad air, garrets and cellars for school-rooms,— everything to produce both physical and mental injury, —are a few only of these features: a much more afflicting characteristic is the want of teachers, of books, and instruction; the very essentials, in fine, of education are wanting (Wyse, 1837, 58).

It was this 'humiliating picture'—and especially the number of children receiving no education at all—that drove middle-class reformers to action, to try to replace the haphazard provision of the voluntary societies by a coherent national system. In this way the late 1830s saw the emergence of the educational pressure group, sometimes national, sometimes local. The creation of the Central Society in London was paralleled by the emergence of Manchester as a focus of educational politics. Liberal-radical Manchester and Salford were actively involved in the late 1830s in the new movement. The Manchester middle-class radicals and liberals, including Richard Cobden, were in touch with Wyse and the parliamentary radicals, as well as with radical educationists elsewhere. Meetings were held in Manchester and Salford in 1837 and an organisation parallel to the Central Society in London was formed, with the backing of a range of liberal, nonconformist and other interests. The meeting which set up the organisation has been described variously as having 2,200 and 4,000 people present (Maltby, 1918, 50; Mumford, 1919, 284). The main speaker of the evening was Thomas Wyse; Brougham had intended to be present but was unable to be so, and another speaker was Samuel Wilderspin, the infant school promoter. The Manchester Society for Promoting National Education was active until 1842, and was important in demonstrating the need for organised middle-class effort in education, effort which was to become of greater importance later in the decade with the creation of the Lancashire (and then the National) Public School Association.

Education and the state

Middle-class radical opinion was now firmly directed towards extending action for working-class education—though opinion was not united as to the means of attaining a national system. The London and Manchester groups, with their allies and spokesmen inside Parliament, exerted strong and influential pressure (with the support of the *Westminster Review*) for a national system of compulsory education. It is against the background of such pressure that the creation of the Committee of Privy Council in 1839 has to be seen. The Committee of Council, wrote a leading member of the main educational pressure group of the 1860s and 1870s—the National Education League—had

> undoubtedly been led up to by the exertions of the Central Society of Education, which, by its agitation, had increased the pressure out of doors, and compelled the Government to take action. It was the motion of Mr. Wyse, the Chairman of the Society, in the former Session, which had forced the hand of the Ministry. It had been intimated to the Society that their zeal embarrassed the Government (Adams, 1882, 105).

The creation of the Committee of Council, whilst introducing a system of supervision of educational expenditure, creating an inspectorate, and strengthening secular control over educational development, was a much smaller step towards a national system than the education societies were demanding.

Differences of opinion over the form and extent of national intervention in education were sharpened by the controversy over Sir James Graham's factory bill of 1843, which contained a scheme for the education of children in workhouses and those employed in textile manufacture. Nonconformist opinion was profoundly hostile to the bill, and widespread agitation was organised against it, largely because of the power it gave the established Church in the appointment of teachers. Only rare radicals were prepared to give Graham's bill even lukewarm support, and J. A. Roebuck clashed with his nonconformist and liberal constituents for doing so (Leader, 1897, 148-9). In the early 1840s, under pressure for social, political and educational improvements, middle-class radicals had to face hostility from within the middle class no less severe than in earlier periods of attempts at reform. The conflict over the 1843 bill (which failed, and was followed by a factory act the following year which omitted the contentious education clauses) led to an influential body of nonconformist opinion adopting a 'voluntaryist' position, rejecting even the level of government involvement in education that had been reached since 1833, and seeking to free the schools from every kind of government support or control. Difficulties in securing educational advances were encountered both in the shape of conservative resistance (often locally organised to oppose educational pressure groups—as in Manchester), and in the different and changing preoccupations of Whig, liberal, radical and nonconformist educationists themselves.

Education and social protection

The awareness among middle-class radicals in the late 1830s and 1840s of the depth of the social crisis, and their search for remedies, took them not only into the problem of extending popular schooling, but also into a range of other formal and informal educational ventures. The radical reformers enthusiastically welcomed, for example, the introduction of the penny postage in 1840, as conducive to educational progress. The reforming pamphleteer, the Rev. Thomas Spencer, wrote in 1843 of Rowland Hill's penny postage that it encouraged learning:

Those who formerly learned to write found their writing of little use, because they could not afford to pay the postage of letters; but when they find that writing is useful to them, the practice of it will become general, and will tend to the improvement of the people. On a similar principle, let the legislature repeal the stamp duty on newspapers ... with all their imperfections, newspapers are the civilizers and instructors of our land, and he is no friend to the people who tries to keep newspapers from them (Spencer, 1843, 14).

Francis Adams called the penny postage 'a most powerful incident to education' (Adams, 1882, 83). The school, cheap postage, and an untaxed press were seen as agencies of social advance because they were 'civilizers' and 'instructors'. There was already profoundly at work among middle-class radicals a sense (that was to receive greater publicity in the period of the 1870 Education Act) that progress towards greater political freedom needed the prior security of an educated and enlightened populace.

This was particularly true after the emergence of Chartism as a political force, and was fundamental to the attitude of many radical reformers. The notion of education as a defence against misguided popular agitation and organisation was expressed most clearly by Benthamite Dr James Kay, later Sir James Kay-Shuttleworth, first secretary of the Committee of Privy Council on Education. He was deeply committed to educational reform and to an enhanced role for the state in the provision of education. From his appointment to the Committee in 1839 he warned strongly of the causal link between ignorance and social disorder. Machine-breakers had 'ignorantly attempted to destroy the chief sources of their own domestic well-being'; the trade unions had by their actions rendered the working classes 'the victims of their ignorance'. Both were 'examples of a class of evils which arise from ignorance', and it was right that the British legislature had decided to resist such evils by relying 'rather on the growth of intelligence among the great body of the people, than on the coercive powers of the law' (Kay-Shuttleworth, 1846, 14-15). In 1839 he related the Chartist petition to the previous thirty years of agitation in various forms, all showing 'how readily masses of ignorance, discontent, and suffering may be misled'. Chartism was, in his eyes, 'an armed political monster'. It had an anarchical spirit which was a threat to the country, and its leaders were 'ignorant' and 'unprincipled'. He was astonished that Conservatives had not taken the lead 'in promoting the diffusion of that knowledge among the working classes which tends beyond any thing else to promote the security of property and the maintenance of public order' (Kay-Shuttleworth, 1862, 229-32). In the late 1830s and 1840s Kay-Shuttleworth was doing no more than express precisely the search for social protection which underlay most of Whig and much of middle-class radical educational thinking.

The commitment of the middle-class radicals to educational expansion and reform, therefore, often contained a degree of condescension, a notion that education was a cheaper and more effective form of social protection than prisons and punishment, but often also a sense of genuine sympathy with poverty and ignorance and their social consequences. Often the middle-class radical motive was a combination of some or all of these—and other—elements. When Quaker liberal Thomas Sturge launched an adult school movement in Birmingham in 1845 to teach young men and women to read the scriptures and to write, and when middle-class radicals like William Ellis supported Chartist William Lovett in his educational plans, it is not always easy to disentangle the various elements present in their motives. There was philanthropy, Christian or utilitarian ideology, a sense of urgency in tackling social problems, a sense of the inherent rightness of education.

97

From nonconformity in particular many middle-class radicals drew some of the energies we have earlier seen influencing educational movements. Nonconformist radicals had no monopoly of enthusiasm for education, but it is important to recognise the continuing nonconformist impact not only on schooling but also and mainly on the search for social solutions, including the strong interest in education.

The endowed schools and the universities

The radical attack on the endowed schools was overshadowed in the 1840s by the preoccupation with popular education. In the late 1830s and early 1840s the public schools were to some extent shielded against criticism by the changes commonly associated with the work of Thomas Arnold at Rugby. Criticism focused more sharply on the local grammar schools, most of which continued in the same kind of intellectual paralysis as in earlier decades. The main burden of the criticism was that the grammar schools were unable or unwilling to take account of the changing world around them. In 1837 Thomas Wyse expressed a view which was widespread in the 1830s and 1840s, and from which we have quoted earlier. If British, National and other schools failed to prepare children for their future occupations and duties,

we find in the Grammar schools much greater defects. The middle class, in all its sections, except the more learned professions, find no instruction which can suit their special middle-class wants. They are fed with the dry husks of ancient learning, when they should be taking sound and substantial food from the great treasury of modern discovery.

It was in the proprietary schools such as University College School, the Proprietary College at Bristol, and similar schools in the City of London and Liverpool that Wyse saw the future (Wyse, 1837, 59-62). Not until the 1860s, however, was discontent with the public and endowed grammar schools to result in government action, in the shape of the Clarendon and Taunton commissions.

In the late 1830s and 1840s criticism of the universities of Oxford and Cambridge had a sharper edge, and demands for university reform continued unabated. There were attempts in Parliament to appoint commissions of inquiry into the two universities. University reform bills were presented in Parliament in 1843 and 1845, and pressure was sustained until the successful appointment of commissions of inquiry in 1850. The pressure for reform came from nonconformists and radicals, their demands focusing on the removal of religious tests. Throughout the 1840s the question of university reform was in one historian's words a 'hardy annual' in Parliament, the outcome of 'links between the academic liberals and dissenters' (Ward, 1965, 127). With strong resistance from the universities, the commissions were appointed, and two years later produced reports which criticised every aspect of the work and organisation of the two universities, and led to substantial changes.

Tory radicalism

What we have seen so far in the 1830s and 1840s is the response to social and educational issues mainly of the political (and utilitarian or philosophic) radicals. Radicals of this kind had found their political positions increasingly conditioned by working-class responses and organisation. The middle-class reformers met with deep working-class suspicion and hostility over the Poor Law Amendment Act of 1834 and subsequent attempts to implement it, and they were frequently identified with the manufacturers against whom much Chartist and other working-class energy was directed. It was issues such as the Poor Law, working hours and factory conditions, that often made it difficult for middle-class and working-class radicals to make common cause. Since Chartism itself was an amalgam of resentments against industrial and urban conditions, as well as a political movement, attempts to harmonise working-class and middle-class radical attitudes often foundered on middle-class radical support for *laissez-faire* doctrines, and on their failure to support attempts to legislate for shorter working hours or to protect children in factories. It was the *laissez-faire* approach of many middle-class radicals in relation to industry, and their identification with the manufacturing interest, which make the emergence of 'Tory radicalism' of importance.

Thomas Carlyle was described in 1840 as a Tory-Radical, 'which is the approved name, with a certain party, for every man of large views and liberal sentiments, who does not place implicit faith for social salvation, only through the Bed-Chamber Whigs'. His was a Toryism of a new type—a 'kind of heroic Toryism, or intellectual and philosophic Feudalism', though the account admitted it was not quite accurate to describe Carlyle as a radical—'he is, at best, on some points, scarce a half Radical' (*Tait's Edinburgh Magazine*, vol. VII, 1840, 115). Carlyle's very individual position nevertheless does express the basis of the 'half radical' position of the influential group of Tories who emerged in strong opposition to factory conditions, to the manufacturers, and in support of and in alliance with the Chartist movement. Describing the 'condition-of-England' question in his *Chartism*, Carlyle laid a great deal of blame at the door of the utilitarians and political radicals. The reformed Parliament had scarcely discussed working-class conditions: they had discussed everything but this 'alpha and omega of all'. Why had Parliament ignored it?

> Radical Members, above all; friends of the people; chosen with effort, by the people, to interpret and articulate the dumb deep want of the people! To a remote observer they seem oblivious of their duty.... They are either speakers for that great dumb toiling class which cannot speak, or they are nothing that one can well specify.

Parliamentary radicalism, Carlyle stormed with his unique brand of thunder, had failed to voice the popular discontent:

> How Parliamentary Radicalism has fulfilled this mission, entrusted to its management these eight years now, is known to all men. The expectant millions have sat at a feast of the Barmecide; been bidden fill themselves with the imagination of meat.

The reason for the radical failure was Benthamite *laissez-faire* 'donothingism': radicalism had become 'Paralytic Radicalism', which

> gauges with Statistic measuring-reed, sounds with Philosophic Politico-Economic plummet the deep dark sea of troubles; and having taught us rightly what an infinite sea of troubles it is, sums up ... that nothing whatever can be done in it by man (Carlyle, 1840, 5, 55-8).

If the manufacturers, the Whigs, the radicals, the parliamentary reformers had disrupted traditional England and failed to solve the problems of the society they had created, only a brand of 'heroic Toryism' could restore social order and justice. Education for Carlyle 'should need no advocating', and he contemptuously dismissed the querulous advocacy of dissenters and churchmen of their own schemes of education. What was needed was a profoundly religious education—not rote, catechismic education for which Birmingham could easily produce droning machines to set up on street corners, but the teaching of religion by a teacher who '*has* religion'. It was not money and repetition of liturgies that made education: 'soul is kindled only by soul' (*ibid.*, 58-62).

Something of this range of attitudes underlies the activities of men like Richard Oastler and the Rev. Joseph Rayner Stephens, who became influential figures in the factory and Chartist movements. They were not radicals in the sense that we have used hitherto; they were dedicated to the restoration of the values of traditional, rural England; they were in favour of restoring to the Church what they saw as its proper role as protector and educator of the poor; they were in favour of the old social order; they were Tories. But they were radical also in that they were able from this position, and at this moment in time, to sympathise with popular discontent, to identify with it and work on its behalf, and in some cases went even so far as to advocate revolutionary positions with the aim of overthrowing the power of the mercantile and industrial interests which they believed were destroying England. They were to be found not only supporting working-class movements, but in their leadership. Many local clergy, especially in the industrial districts, played an important part in the movement for factory reform, even if they did not press their support, as did Stephens for example, within the Chartist ranks.

Richard Oastler championed the cause of the factory

children from the early 1830s, was prominent in the ten-hour movement, and identified himself closely with the Chartist movement, though always with reservations about its precise political aims. In 1837 the Working Men's Association made him an honorary member (Howell, 1970, 66, 83). Tories like Oastler, Stephens, John Fielden and Lord Shaftesbury played a part of one kind or another in movements for social reform in the 1830s and 1840s, but it was Oastler and Stephens who most prominently influenced the Chartist agitation, defiantly challenging the authorities and frequently advocating violent measures. It is understandable, against this background, that Oastler saw education as subsidiary to the fight against what he called 'the Factory Monster'. Education was in his view 'under the present unregulated manufacturing system ... worse than useless'. There was no point in trying to educate the people without giving them time for education. Mill-owners who had been prominent in the fight for the emancipation of the slaves were the most violent opponents of attempts to reform factory slavery (*Fleet Papers*, vol. I, no. 4, 1841, 26; vol. I, no. 5, 1841, 11; vol. II, no. 17, 1842, 134). Oastler represented, therefore, a different kind of radical voice, one which sympathised with popular suffering, allied himself with radical agitation, but pursued objectives which were ultimately far different from those of the working-class political radicals. He sought to restore the rights of the church as well as of the poor; he wanted education, but in the hands of the church; he denounced the Committee of Council and saw compulsory education as an injustice under the prevailing organisation of society; he was contemptuous of dissenters, as the mainstay of the factory system and as opponents of attempts to legislate on behalf of the factory children. He opposed the 1843 factory bill because it was unchristian and unjust to the poor—not because it was unfair to the dissenters. When the bill was abandoned he thanked God (*ibid.*, vol. III, no. 21, 1843, 161-7; vol. III, no. 22, 1843, 169; vol. III, no. 27, 1843, 209).

Middle-class radicalism in the 1840s

The anxieties and tensions of industrial England in the 1830s and 1840s had made 'middle-class radicalism' less easy to define. Politically the radicals were still those who looked to reform of and through Parliament, to the strengthening of parliamentary control over and provision of education, to the extension of justice and democracy. Socially, the measures of reform fought for in Parliament by Tory Radicals and evangelicals like Lord Shaftesbury, and outside Parliament by men like Richard Oastler, were often of equal or greater significance. The fight to prevent child factory labour, to reduce working hours, for adequate and dignified poor relief, for the improvement of housing conditions—all of these were in their context as important to the radical reform of society and of education as any of the objectives pursued by middle-class radicals—including that of popular education itself. For economic and political reasons middle-class radicalism was unable to embrace a programme of both political and social reform as coherent as that of the majority of working-class radicals and Chartists. At different times in the 1830s and 1840s working-class radical movements found themselves in alliance with different kinds of middle-class radical for different purposes—parliamentary reform, co-operative communities, factory reform, and others. The alliances were often hesitant and short-lived. A constant theme of discussion in both middle-class and working-class radical movements was the question of identifying allies, judging how far alliances could be reliable and profitable, estimating the sincerity of would-be allies, patching up quarrels, working out or rejecting compromises.

By the 1840s England had a Committee of the Privy Council to supervise the spending of the growing parliamentary grant, inspectors of schools, factory acts which had introduced a system of half-time education for children in the textile factories, factory inspectors, and widespread disagreement about the means of extending education for the poor and of reforming the endowed and public schools and ancient universities. There were also pressure groups, educational programmes, movements to restore the voluntary principle in education, and movements to establish a nation-wide and compulsory system of education. Education was an inescapable topic of discussion in radical publications and programmes, and radicals and radical movements of various kinds had become engaged in educational experiments and plans—for everything from early infant education to adult education. While radicals were primarily concerned, in their different ways, with working out a new political destiny for increasingly industrial Britain, they were turning the discussion in detail to that of the national system for which explicit demands were being made.

Radicalism and education at mid-century

Late Chartism and education

The years 1848-50 were of considerable importance in the story of radicalism and its relationship to education. In them Chartism reached its climax, and its energies began to be diverted into other channels; middle-class Christian socialism appeared; the movement for national, secular education, which had started in 1847 as the Lancashire Public School Association, became the National Public School Association in 1850; Marx and Engels's *Communist Manifesto*, published in German in 1848, appeared in English in 1850; trade unionism was strengthened by the 'new model' unionism which was signalled by the creation of the Amalgamated Society of Engineers in 1850. Political contours were changing. Education remained central to the debates of social and political movements: 'educational discussions', wrote a clergyman in 1850, 'have of late been as frequent and as fierce as theological discussions' (Green, 1850, 51).

The movement whose impact and implications were still being most keenly felt at the end of the 1840s was Chartism, although its last appearance as a mass movement was in 1848. Historians have not found it easy to assess the outcomes of Chartism, given that its basic political demand was not won until the reform acts of 1867 and 1884, and that its political programme disguised a range of social objectives. The zig-zags of social movements and changes make it difficult to relate the two. Later organised working-class politics drew strengths from the traditions which were embodied in Chartism. A historian of Scottish Chartism makes the point that 'education is cumulative and has no real yard-stick for measuring progress. Probably the first fruits of enlightened Scottish Chartism were reaped by the Socialist movement after 1850' (Wright, 1953, 103). Another view of the effect of Chartism generally is that it 'made the upper and middle classes aware of the wage-earning classes with a distinctness that left no debate as to the latent power residing in the laboring masses. It is possible that the chief result of the whole Chartist effort was just this fact' (Gillespie, 1927, 4). Chartism after 1848 was not only the story of the 1851 Chartist convention and the precise nature of Chartist efforts in the movement's final phase, but also the story of the activities of ex-Chartists, the new directions of working-class activity, and above all the reality of its 'latent power' in the consciousness of mid-Victorian Britain.

Although the Chartist movement declined after the demonstration of April 1848, the grass roots interest in education it had encouraged continued to find expression in many ways. William Lovett, who withdrew from the London Working Men's Association in 1847, two years before it collapsed, continued to run the Holborn Hall school into the late 1850s and became a strong advocate of elementary anatomy and physiology in schools, and taught them himself. In his book on *Social and Political Morality*, published in 1853, he argued even more firmly than in the 1840 programme for a national system of education, and for this he was convinced that 'an act of legislature is needed'. The aim was the establishment and maintenance in every district of

> a sufficient number (according to the population) of infant, preparatory, high, normal, and reformatory schools; to which the children of the district shall have free access.... The establishment ... of a wise and just system of education formed for, and controlled by, the people, cannot be much longer delayed.

Children were to be taught, among other things, about their own bodies and about the government of society, and education would soon be seen 'as an instrument of individual, social and political regeneration and happiness' (Lovett, 1853, 137-42).

Thomas Cooper, expelled from the Chartist convention of 1846 amidst deep internal divisions, remained an influential figure. Among other activities in the late 1840s he edited the *Plain Speaker* and *Cooper's Journal* in 1849 and 1850, advocating pressure for reform through individual petitions, the settlement of waste lands, and above all self-education and the formation of societies for educational mutual aid. Cooper retained the conviction in the power of education that he had tried to voice at the 1846 convention, and coupled with it a growing interest in co-operative production: 'Association—Association—is the remedy,' he proclaimed in May 1850. In the same year he proposed a Progress Union which would be based on societies for 'mutual instruction and discussion classes, libraries, and weekly lectures', the aim being 'to raise the intellectual and moral condition of the whole community'. His proposals and emphases have to be seen against the background of disappointment with the failure of other, formal educational agencies, and of the mass Chartist movement itself. In the first issues of *Cooper's Journal* he wrote:

What, then, can we do, in this year 1850, towards laying a sure and enduring foundation for our great enterprise —the enlightenment and enfranchisement of all? The old Mechanics' Institutes, it is confirmed by their best and worthiest supporters, have failed to accomplish their purpose: the political associations of the working classes have become almost lifeless (*Cooper's Journal*, vol. I, no. 1, 1850, 1; vol. I, no. 20, 1850, 305).

Little is known about the final phase of activity and the disappearance of local Chartist halls and other activities, but independent working-class organisation on these lines certainly continued in the late 1840s and 1850s, with support which included Chartist, Owenite and other energies. When a People's Hall was opened at Hanley, in the Potteries, in 1850, its announced objective was the establishment of a building 'for social, educational and political uses'. A supporter explained that the aim was 'to unite in one body all who were desirous to promote the political and social improvement of the people'. It was to provide a home for the trades societies, an alternative to the Mechanics' Institute, a good library and reading room and schools for working-class boys and girls. Its historian explains that it 'identified itself closely with Chartism. It derived in part from radical politics and part from working-class disillusionment with the Potteries Mechanics Institution' (Lowe, 1972, 77). The 1851 Chartist convention, as we have seen, discussed education, and even the last conference of the movement in 1858 heard an address from Robert Owen (who died later that year), in which he was still urging the provision of a 'highly beneficial education' for the working class (West, 1920, 274; see also Wilson, 1887, 25).

Chartism, it has been suggested, produced ideas which could as easily lead into liberalism as into socialism (White,

1965, 13; Harrison and Hollis, 1967, 505). Working-class forms of radical action, including in relation to education, constitute a clear tradition in the first half of the century, and in very different economic and political conditions after mid-century this tradition forms a less coherent thread. Discussion of the bridges across from Chartism to liberalism or the socialism of the 1880s is a different process from the discussion of the early decades of working-class radical organisation. After mid-century radicals of all kinds had to respond to changing conditions and take different initiatives—but to people's awareness at mid-century of the working class and its social and political ideals Chartism had made a crucial contribution.

Christian Socialism

Amid the uncertainties which followed the 1848 Chartist agitation, and as a reaction against it, emerged the short-lived radical-conservative movement of Christian Socialism, advocating a form of co-operation, essentially under aristocratic guidance. With something of the Tory-radical antipathy to industrial and commercial values, the Christian Socialists were—unlike the Tory radicals—hostile to political action, and isolated from any form of popular movement. The first issue of the group's *Politics for the People* in May 1848 contained a letter to the Chartists (written anonymously by Charles Kingsley), explaining that the Chartists had made 'the same mistake as the rich of whom you complain ... the mistake of fancying that legislative reform is social reform, or that men's hearts can be changed by act of parliament'. The basic aim of the group was to influence working-class action away from political agitation. The Chartists had been 'trying to do God's work with the devil's tools' (*Politics for the People*, no. 1, 1848,

29). Using the model of a People's College which had been set up in Sheffield in 1842, the Christian Socialists—F. D. Maurice in particular—were also to turn to adult education, and with the creation of the London Working Men's College in 1854 were to give a new impetus to the movement. The Christian Socialists were radical only in the sense that they recognised the existence of serious social problems and looked for forms of action—but for them all social and political problems became moral problems, manifestations of evil, and 'Christianity is the only power on earth which has ever imposed as a law this total extinction of evil'. Their radicalism was what J. M. Ludlow, one of the group, described as 'the radicalism of Christianity' (*ibid.*, no. 13, 1848, 221-2). The many discussions of education in the pages of the group's journal amounted entirely to a plea for education to be based on Christian values, though the journal offered no programme for its provision. Christian Socialism did not mesh in with popular radicalism and action as Tory radicalism had done.

Owenism after the 1830s

Although in the late 1830s and 1840s Chartism was the focal point of radical pressures, Owenism continued to play an important, though changed, role. From the collapse of Owenism as in any sense a mass movement in 1834 the Owenites had developed a variety of active organisations, always rationalist, secularist and 'socialist', and always devoting their organisation and propaganda to the pursuit of community, a rational society and a rational education. The outstanding Owenite community venture at Queenwood, in Hampshire, began in 1839. Owen's reiteration of his doctrines continued unabated through the 1840s. Owenite Halls of Science played an important part in the continued radical educational efforts of popular movements; among other things they 'challenged the social and economic assumptions of orthodox mechanics' institutes. Much general educational work was included in the programme of these organisations' (Tylecote, 1957, 125). The Rational Religionists, as the Owenite organisation was called from 1839, devoted considerable efforts to opening such halls of science (or 'social institutions'), and in 1840 halls had either opened or were under construction in Sheffield, London, Manchester, Huddersfield, Liverpool, Birmingham, Coventry, Bradford, Glasgow and many other towns (Podmore, 1906, 469-70). The Liverpool Owenites opened a juvenile school of science in 1841, and a Workers' Educational Institute was created at the Sheffield Hall of Science in 1847 (Rose, 1957, 176-7; Salt, 1971, 196). At a dinner following the laying of the foundation stone for a hall of science in Manchester in 1839 the toasts included one to the Queen, hoping that her reign would 'be distinguished by the speedy emancipation of her sex from the barbaric slavery of their present social and political disqualification' (*Temple of Free Enquiry*, 1839, 14). This was reported as being followed by 'much cheering'. Another toast read: 'may equal means of education be provided for every individual of the State without distinction of sex, sect, class or party' (*ibid.*, 27). Owenism in the 1830s and 1840s was one of the movements most alert to the position of women and to the education of girls.

By the late 1840s Owenite activities were declining—though information as to the precise scale of Owenite activity in this phase is scarce, and the rate of decline of local activities is unclear. Owenite efforts in the 1830s and 1840s had also been related to other communitarian or utopian groups and ideals. In education, continental influence—mainly that of Pestalozzi—was being mediated into British experience. Utopian radical J. P. Greaves, who published a series of letters from Pestalozzi, died in a community at Ham Common, Surrey, in 1842. An obituary in a communitarian journal described his contact with Pestalozzi, following which Greaves had 'had a continual bias towards Progressive Education. He seemed to have appreciated the spirit that animated Pestalozzi, in its fullest sense, hence his eminent success in arousing in all his disciples the true Educational Idea' (*Educational Circular and Communist Apostle*, no. 2, n.s., 1841, 46). The communitarian movement absorbed energies and ideals other than those of Owen, but his message was the most powerful one of the 1830s and 1840s. His new view of society had a lasting hold, even within the context of other and even rival movements: 'when all his schemes had ended in bankruptcy, there were men prepared to continue his work' (Dobbs, 1919, 220). In terms of practical educational activity this became particularly true of the work of the new co-operative movement—identified with the Rochdale Equitable Pioneers, whose educational work began effectively in 1849. The Rochdale co-operators had begun in 1844 to adapt the Owenite ideal to more immediate, practicable aims—to establish not communities but a form of co-operative trading. Many of the Rochdale co-operators from the beginning met for discussion in the room behind the store. In 1848 they obtained premises large enough to launch educational work. They appointed a committee and collected subscriptions of twopence a month. A reading room was opened with newspapers and magazines (free to all members of the society, whether or not subscribers to the 'Educational Department'). They sold books, newspapers and periodicals and devoted the profits to the library. The library (supported also by donations from the Society and later by a proportion of profits) was open at the beginning on Saturday evenings. By the mid-1850s it had over 1,000 volumes, opened on other evenings, and then began to issue catalogues and obtain equipment such as globes and telescopes (Greenwood, 1877, 5-7). The Rochdale model of a reading room and an educational fund set aside by the parent society was followed by other co-operative organisations, and out of these beginnings grew the extensive educational work of the co-operative movement in the late nineteenth and twentieth centuries.

Social science and secular schools

The most important of the middle-class movements at the end of the 1840s, which contained radicals and sought radical aims in education, were those connected with the secular school movement and with the Lancashire Public School Association. The outstanding secular school proponents had relations both with phrenology and with utilitarianism. Of central importance was the work of George Combe, phrenologist and educationist, whose book on *The Constitution of Man* was first published in 1828, and was frequently reprinted as one of the influential books of the nineteenth century. William Ellis, Benthamite radical and friend of John Stuart Mill, read the book and as a result in 1846 began to advocate the teaching of social science and to found schools which would be secular, and with a curriculum rooted in social science and physiology. He supported Lovett in beginning such a school at the Holborn Hall in 1848—and Ellis himself taught elementary social science there (Robinson, 1919, 65-9; Lovett, 1876, II, 368-81). Also in 1848 Ellis opened the first of his Birkbeck schools on the premises of the London Mechanics' Institution, and at the same time Combe, James Simpson and others were opening the Williams' Secular School in Edinburgh, where Combe taught phrenology and physiology (Jolly, 1879, xxii-xxiii). The number of such schools increased at the end of the 1840s and in the early 1850s, including at Manchester, Birmingham, Glasgow and Leith —often with Ellis's financial support. The curriculum invariably contained some kind of social science and natural science, physiology and often phrenology. The social science was in essence simple political economy, and Ellis, Combe, W. B. Hodgson (secretary of the Liverpool Mechanics' Institute from 1839 and later professor of economics at Edinburgh) and others campaigned for the teaching of the laws of economic and industrial life in schools. Hodgson in 1854 was lecturing at the Royal Institution on economic science as a branch of education, and through the 1860s and into the 1870s he and Ellis lectured and wrote widely on the subject. By 1852 eight 'Birkbeck' schools in London and three similar ones elsewhere had been founded by Ellis or with his financial assistance (Robinson, 1919, 83). Only the last of Ellis's schools, founded in 1862, was to survive into the twentieth century (as William Ellis School, in North London).

Essential to the work of this group of educators was the notion of secular education. James Simpson, one of the most active of them, summarised the nature and implications of this outlook in a campaigning speech on the subject of national education (at a meeting which he shared with Combe) in Aberdeen in 1851. Secular education

consists in realities instead of mere words, which alone are taught in the old-fashioned schools. . . . Secular instruction, in its widest sense, embraces all that is known of this temporal world, material and moral. . . . Do any of my hearers doubt that such an institution is realizable in a secular school? I will refer them to the Birkbeck schools in London, where 1500 young persons of both sexes are receiving, most successfully, all its benefits; 150 are reaping the same advantage in Mr. Williams' secular school in Edinburgh (*Report of the Proceedings*, 1851, 6).

This outlook and this experience coincided with the foundation of the Lancashire Public School Association in Manchester in 1847, and some of the secularists, mainly Simpson and Hodgson, played an important part in it.

The Lancashire Public School Association

The LPSA was created on the basis of a plan 'for the establishment of a general system of secular education in the County of Lancaster'. Under this plan education was to be available for all, and 'the most effectual barriers should be provided against the introduction of sectarian teaching'. Every parish or township in the county was to appoint a committee annually, to establish and provide out of the rates common day schools for children from five to fifteen, evening, infant and industrial schools. A county board of education would be established among other things to supervise the appointment of competent teachers. The plan discussed in detail the admission of selections from the scriptures into the schools, but by such means as would prevent 'sectarian teaching' (Jolly, 1879, 719-29). When, in 1850, the organisation was turned into a National Association, there was a dispute about whether it should be described as in favour of 'secular' or 'non-sectarian' education—though in the event the word 'public' was retained in the title (Maltby, 1918, 78-9). John Stuart Mill angrily protested at the dilution of the Association's aims by the omission of the word 'secular', at the fact that it had

> let itself be persuaded by Mr. Cobden, aided by some dissenting ministers, to sacrifice its distinctive flag, and instead of calling itself an Association for secular education should have sheltered its timidity under the ambiguous designation of unsectarian ... if you could carry all the sects with you by your compromise you would have effected nothing but a compact among the more powerful bodies to cease fighting among themselves and join in trampling on the weaker (Mill, 1873, 326-8).

The Association absorbed some of the organisation and energies of the recently dissolved Anti-Corn Law League; meetings were held from 1850 all over the country, and local branches were formed. The *Westminster Review* supported the new organisation, which conducted agitation, sponsored parliamentary action—including education bills, and remained active until the mid-1850s, and existed until 1862. It has been pointed out that all the major education debates and proposals of the late nineteenth and early twentieth centuries 'may be found in the annals of the L.P.S.A. and the N.P.S.A. between 1848 and 1851' (Maltby, 1918, 67).

Middle-class and working-class radicalism

By the middle of the nineteenth century educational debate had focused more and more sharply on the role of the state and the need for a more extensive and efficient system than was possible under the voluntary system. Religious and ideological rivalries were still pronounced, and the suspicions engendered by confrontations such as those of 1843 remained barriers to advance. Middle-class radicals had by now, however, learned to organise educational pressure groups on a substantial scale, and in the events leading up to the 1870 Education Act this aspect of the middle-class tradition was to be of major importance. The tradition of middle-class radical involvement in the dissemination of 'useful knowledge' was also to remain important. The Christian Socialist movement led into the idea of working men's colleges, and the interest of a radical Quaker in Birmingham at the end of the 1840s led to a slow revival of the earlier interest in adult schools.

The main interest in radicalism and education at mid-century must focus, however, on the changes taking place in working-class organisation and in working-class ideas relating to education. Economic, social and political conditions were changing. The political tensions of the 1840s eased as economic problems became less acute. In 1846, with some optimism, George Combe wrote that he had 'never known England and Scotland, morally and physically, in a more promising condition' (Gibbon, 1878, II, 213). Whatever the improvements, it is unlikely that the majority of working men were so enthusiastic. In a tone of voice that is reminiscent of Paine, Owen and popular radicalism of earlier decades, Thomas Cooper wrote in 1849 that a new era was at hand—a different kind of optimism, which reflected the events of June 1848 in France. Revolutions, wrote Cooper, had generally been effected by minorities, often by winning support from the 'inferior' classes:

Now, an entire social change is about to be introduced, and the attempt to remedy the inequality which has existed for ages is about to be made by the 'inferior' classes. This cannot be long delayed. The present year may furnish a chapter more startling than the preface of the last (*Plain Speaker*, vol. I, no. 1, 20 January 1849, 6). The tradition of independent working-class education remained strong, and any such expectation of the millennium did not interfere with continuing efforts at self and mutual improvement. Nor did it prevent the Miners' Association in 1847 from petitioning Parliament for an extension of the educational provisions introduced under the factory acts (Dobbs, 1919, 230; Robson, 1931, 151). In the event, Cooper's optimism was proved wrong. Working-class action to remedy inequality continued, though in different forms, with different emphases, and often with more limited objectives. The most characteristic form of action in the 1850s was to be that of the trade-union organisations of the more skilled workers.

Education and class structure

At mid-century acceptance of the class structure of industrial English society was complete, and all action for education reflected this consciousness of profound class divisions. A prize essay published in 1850 (the judges included Quaker radical Edward Miall and the reforming pamphleteer, the Rev. Thomas Spencer) postulated, in terms accepted generally by mid-Victorian Britain: 'that there must be a working class, in distinction from the class of employers and capitalists, I assume as an established truth ... let each class of the community, then, understand its true position'. Glossing over the political divisions and tensions of recent years the writer, the Rev. Samuel Green, pointed to the particular phenomenon of the urban working class:

The masses of working people congregated in the metropolis, our larger seaports, and the factories and mines of the north, possess a far more marked and decided character. Their association, and often their employment, creates a large amount of intellectual energy. Education, consequently, is much more general.... The notion, prevalent so long, of the superior morality of rural districts is now fairly dispelled by the strong evidence of facts (Green, 1850, 4-6, 20).

The consciousness of mid-century Britain ranged from such an acceptance of the 'intellectual energy' of the industrial and urban working class to a sense of its latent power or danger.

In educational terms this meant a widespread middle-class awareness that only extended and improved popular education could avert the dangers of class division. In 1857 the *Newcastle Weekly Chronicle* was deploring 'the startling fact that education has yet done little to remove the barriers of prejudice and ignorance which separate class from class in this country' (Burn, 1964, 110-11). Class, it was assumed, was inevitable and natural—prejudice was not. On the opposing side of the divide, Marx and Engels were describing education in 1848 (in English in G. J. Harney's *Red Republican* in 1850), as determined by social conditions: 'The Communists have not invented the intervention of society in education; they do but seek to alter the character of that intervention, and to rescue education from the influence of the ruling class' (Marx and Engels, 1848, 25). Education was being interpreted not only as a socially necessary instrument for harnessing working-class 'intellectual energy' but also as a weapon in the hands of one class or another. From the London Corresponding Society of the 1790s, through the variety of radical forms of the first half of the nineteenth century, education had remained a vital part of political and social debate and action.

Suggestions for further reading

The best approach to the history of the period covered in
this book is through Elie Halévy's series of books on the
history of the English people in the nineteenth century, of
which the most relevant is *The Liberal Awakening 1815-
1830* (1926). His *The Growth of Philosophic Radicalism*
(1928) is a good starting point for further work on those
aspects of middle-class radicalism discussed here. For popular and working-class radicalism in the period up to about
1830 the best account is Edward Thompson's *The Making
of the English Working Class* (1963). The educational programmes, ideas and activities of radical movements are
discussed in the pioneer and still extremely valuable *Education and Social Movements 1700-1850* (1919) by A. E.
Dobbs. A detailed discussion of this period can be found in
Brian Simon's important *Studies in the History of Education 1780-1870* (1960), and relevant extracts from some of
the people whose ideas are discussed here are contained in
his *The Radical Tradition in Education in Britain* (1972).
My own *The Concept of Popular Education* (1965) discusses
education and social movements mainly in the 1820s and
1830s. Two books by R. F. Wearmouth, *Methodism and
the Working-Class Movements of England 1800-1850*

(1937) and *Some Working-Class Movements of the Nineteenth Century* (1948), contain important accounts of the tradition of political and educational 'class meetings'.

Systematic accounts of the educational content of some of the social and political movements discussed here remain to be written. On the educational work and impact of Chartism, for example, there is no detailed study to recommend, and the autobiographies of William Lovett and Thomas Cooper remain the best starting points. A flavour of the role of radical movements in overall developments can be obtained from Maltby's case study of *Manchester and the Movement for National Elementary Education 1800-1870* (1918). On specific themes the reader will have to follow the clues in references in the text, in the bibliography, and in the books recommended above.

Bibliography

The first date of publication is given in all cases. Mention of a later edition indicates the one to which reference is made in the text. The place of publication is London unless otherwise stated.

ADAMS, FRANCIS (1882), *History of the Elementary School Contest in England*, Chapman & Hall.

AKENSIDE, DONALD H. (1970), *The Irish Education Experiment*, Routledge & Kegan Paul.

ALDRICH, RICHARD EDWARD (1970), 'Education and the Political Parties, 1830-1870', London University M.Phil. thesis.

ALDRICH, R. E. (1973), 'Radicalism, National Education and the Grant of 1833', *Journal of Educational Administration and History*, vol. V, no. 1.

ALFRED (1857), *The History of the Factory Movement*, Simpkin, Marshall, 2 vols.

ALISON, ARCHIBALD (1845), *England in 1815 and 1845*, Edinburgh, Blackwood.

ALTICK, RICHARD D. (1957), *The English Common Reader*, Chicago, University of Chicago Press.

ASPINALL, ARTHUR (1927), *Lord Brougham and the Whig Party*, Manchester, Manchester University Press.

AVELING, EDWARD and AVELING, ELEANOR MARX (1888), *Shelley's Socialism*, published privately (edition of 1947).

BAIN, ALEXANDER (1882), *James Mill*, Longmans, Green.

BIBLIOGRAPHY

BAKER, CHARLES (1837), 'Mechanics' Institutions and Libraries', Central Society of Education, *First Publication*, Taylor & Walton (edition of 1968).

BAKER, C. (1839), 'Infants' Schools', Central Society of Education, *Third Publication*, Taylor & Walton (edition of 1968).

BAMFORD, SAMUEL (1893), *Passages in the Life of a Radical*, Fisher & Unwin.

BARNARD, H. C. (1970), *Were Those the Days? A Victorian Education*, Oxford, Pergamon.

BELLOT, H. HALE (1929), *University College London 1826-1926*, University of London Press.

BERDAHL, ROBERT O. (1957), *British Universities and the State*, Berkeley, University of California Press.

Birmingham Co-operative Herald.

BLACK, A. (1954, 1955), 'Education before Rochdale', two articles, *Co-operative Review*, vol. xxviii, no. 6 and vol. xxix, no. 2.

BLACK, EUGENE CHARLTON (1963), *The Association: British extraparliamentary political organization 1769-1793*, Cambridge, Mass., Harvard University Press.

BRAILSFORD (1949), 'Radical Democracy in the Victorian Era', British Broadcasting Corporation, *Ideas and Beliefs of the Victorians*, Sylvan Press.

BRIGGS, ASA (1956), 'Middle-class Consciousness in English Politics, 1780-1846', *Past and Present*, no. 9.

BROWN, PHILIP ANTHONY (1918), *The French Revolution in English History*, Crosby Lockwood.

BUCKMASTER, J. C. (1862), *The Education Question in Parliament*, Chapman & Hall.

BURN, W. L. (1964), *The Age of Equipoise. A study of the mid-Victorian generation*, Allen & Unwin.

BURSTON, W. H. (ed.) (1969), *James Mill on Education*, Cambridge University Press.

CARLYLE, THOMAS (1840), *Chartism*, Fraser (edition of 1888).

CARLYLE, THOMAS (1843), *Past and Present*, Chapman & Hall (edition of 1888).

CARTWRIGHT, JOHN (1812), *Six Letters to the Marquis of Tavistock, on a Reform of the Commons House of Parliament*, M'Creery.

CARTWRIGHT, JOHN (1776), *Take Your Choice!*, n.p. (edition of 1786).

CENTRAL SOCIETY OF EDUCATION (1838), 'Schools for the Industrious Classes', *Second Publication*, Taylor & Walton (edition of 1968).

CENTRAL SOCIETY OF EDUCATION (1837), 'Statistical Inquiries of the Central Society of Education into the Social Condition of the Working Classes', *First Publication* (edition of 1968).

CESTRE, CHARLES (1906), *John Thelwall, a Pioneer of Democracy and Social Reform in England during the French Revolution*, Swan Sonnenschein.

CHALLINOR, RAYMOND and RIPLEY, BRIAN (1968), *The Miners' Association: a trade union in the age of the Chartists*, Lawrence & Wishart.

CHRISTIE, IAN R. (1962), *Wilkes, Wyvill and Reform: the parliamentary reform movement in British politics 1760-1785*, Macmillan.

CLAXTON, TIMOTHY (1844), *Hints to Mechanics on Self-Education and Mutual Instruction*, Taylor & Walton.

CLIVE, JOHN (1957), *Scotch Reviewers: The Edinburgh Review, 1802-1815*, Faber.

COBBETT, WILLIAM (1829), *Advice to Young Men, and (incidentally) to Young Women, in the Middle and Higher Ranks of Life*, Mills, Jowett & Mills (undated Ward, Lock edition).

COLE, G. D. H. (1953), *Socialist Thought: the forerunners 1789-1850*, Macmillan.

COMBE, GEORGE, *The Constitution of Man considered in Relation to External Objects*, Edinburgh, Anderson, 1828 (edition of 1871).

COOPER, THOMAS (1879), *The Life of Thomas Cooper. Written by himself*, Hodder & Stoughton.

CO-OPERATIVE CONGRESSES, *Reports and Papers, 1831-2* (3-volume collection of documents, Goldsmiths' Library, University of London).

Co-operator.

Cooper's Journal.

COWHERD, RAYMOND G. (1959), *The Politics of English Dissent: the religious aspects of liberal and humanitarian reform movements from 1815 to 1848*, Epworth Press.

CRUSE, AMY (1930), *The Englishman and his Books in the Early Nineteenth Century*, Harrap.

DALY, J. BOWLES (1892), *The Dawn of Radicalism*, Swan Sonnenschein.

DETROSIER, ROWLAND (1829), *An Address delivered at the New Mechanics' Institution, Pool-Street, Manchester ... 1829*, Manchester, Forrest.

DETROSIER, ROWLAND (1831), *An Address on the Advantages of the Intended Mechanics' Hall of Science ... 1831*, Manchester, Hampson & Hadfield.

DETROSIER, R. (1831), *An Address delivered to the Members of the New Mechanics' Institution, Manchester ... 1831, on the necessity of an extension of moral and political instruction among the working classes*, Manchester, Forrest (edition of 1834).

DOBBS, A. E. (1919), *Education and Social Movements 1700-1850*, Longmans, Green.

DORLING, WILLIAM (1879), *Henry Vincent*, n.p.

DRIVER, CECIL (1946), *Tory Radical: the life of Richard Oastler*, New York, Oxford University Press.

EAGLE, E. C. (1958-9), 'The Leicester Mechanics' Institute: 1834-1870—A Re-assessment I', *Bewley House Papers*, vol. iii, no. 7.

Economist: a periodical paper, explanatory of the new system of society projected by Robert Owen.

Edinburgh Review.

Educational Circular and Communist Apostle (1841), no. 2, n.s.

ENGELS, F. (1845, German edition), *The Condition of the Working Class in England*, English edition, eds W. O. Henderson and W. H. Chaloner, Oxford, Blackwell, 1958.

FAULKNER, HAROLD UNDERWOOD (1916), *Chartism and the Churches: a study in democracy*, New York, Columbia College.

FELKIN, F. W. (1909), *From Gower Street to Frognal: a short history of University College School from 1830 to 1907*, Fairbairns.

The Fleet Papers, being letters ... from Richard Oastler.

Fraser's Magazine for Town and Country.

GAMMAGE, R. G. (1854), *History of the Chartist Movement 1837-1854*, Newcastle-upon-Tyne, Browne & Browne (edition of 1894).

GARNETT, R. G. (1963), 'E. T. Craig: communitarian, educator, phrenologist', *Vocational Aspect*, vol. xv.

GIBBON, CHARLES (1878), *The Life of George Combe*, Macmillan, 2 vols.

GIBBS, F. W. (1965), *Joseph Priestley: adventurer in science and champion of truth*, Nelson.

GILBERT, AMY (1922), 'The Work of Lord Brougham for Education in England', Pennsylvania University Ph.D. thesis.

GILLESPIE, FRANCES EMMA (1927), *Labor and Politics in England 1850-1867*, N. Carolina, Duke University Press.

GLASGOW, ERIC (1954), 'The Establishment of the *Northern Star* Newspaper', *History*, no. xxxix, n.s.

GODWIN, WILLIAM (1797), *The Enquirer. Reflections on education, manners, and literature*, n.p.

GODWIN, WILLIAM (1793), *Enquiry concerning Political Justice and its influence on Morals and Happiness*, n.p. (facsimile edition, University of Toronto Press, ed. F. E. L. Priestley, 1946).

GREEN, SAMUEL (1850), *The Working Classes of Great Britain; their present condition, and the means of their improvement and elevation*, Snow.

GREEN, V. H. H. (1957), *Oxford Common Room: a study of Lincoln College and Mark Pattison*, Arnold.

GREEN, V. H. H. (1969), *The Universities*, Harmondsworth, Penguin.

GREENWOOD, A. (1877), *The Educational Department of the Rochdale Equitable Pioneers' Society Limited: its origin and development*, Manchester, Central Co-operative Board.

GREENWOOD, MAUREEN (1973), 'Education and Politics in Leicester: 1828-1850', Leicester University M.Ed. thesis.

GRIFFITH, GEORGE (1867), *The Endowed Schools of England and Ireland, their Past, Present and Future*, Whittaker.

HALÉVY, ELIE (1928), *The Growth of Philosophic Radicalism*, Faber & Gwyer.

HALÉVY, ELIE (1926), *The Liberal Awakening 1815-1830*, Fisher Unwin (edition of 1949).

HALÉVY, ELIE (1956), *Thomas Hodgskin*, Benn.

HAMMOND, H. L. and BARBARA (1930), *The Age of the Chartists 1832-1854: a study of discontent*, Longmans, Green.

HANS, N. (1952), 'Bentham and the Utilitarians', in A. V. Judges (ed.), *Pioneers of English Education*, Faber.

HARRISON, BRIAN and HOLLIS, PATRICIA (1967), 'Chartism, Liberalism and the Life of Robert Lowery', *English Historical Review*, vol. lxxxii.

HARRISON, J. F. C. (1961), *Learning and Living 1790-1960: a study in the history of the English adult education movement*, Routledge & Kegan Paul.

HAZLITT, WILLIAM (1816), *Memoirs of the late Thomas Holcroft*, n.p.

HAZLITT, WILLIAM (1826), *The Plain Speaker*, Colburn (edition of 1928).

HAZLITT, WILLIAM (1825), *The Spirit of the Age*, n.p. (edition of 1928).

HAZLITT, WILLIAM (1819), 'What is the People?', in *Political Essays with Sketches of Public Characters*, n.p.

HILL, MATTHEW DAVENPORT (1822), *Plans for the Government and Liberal Instruction of Boys, in large Numbers; drawn from experience*, Whittaker.

HODGSKIN, THOMAS (1825), *Labour Defended against the Claims of Capital*, n.p. (edition of 1964).

HOLLIS, PATRICIA (1970), *The Pauper Press: a study in working-class radicalism of the 1830s*, Oxford University Press.

HOLYOAKE, GEORGE JACOB (1873), *John Stuart Mill as some of the Working Classes knew him*, Trübner.

HOLYOAKE, GEORGE JACOB (1881), *Life of Joseph Rayner Stephens, Preacher and Political Orator*, Williams & Norgate.

HOPE, ROYDEN BIRTLEY (1947), 'Dr. Thomas Percival, a Medical Pioneer and Social Reformer, 1740-1804', Manchester University M.A. thesis.

HOVELL, MARK (1918), *The Chartist Movement*, Manchester, Manchester University Press.

HOWELL, GEORGE (1972), *A History of the Working Men's Association from 1836 to 1850*, Newcastle-upon-Tyne, Graham.

HUDSON, J. W. (1851), *The History of Adult Education*, n.p.

HYNDMAN, H. M. (1883), *The Historical Basis of Socialism in England*, Kegan Paul, Trench.

JAMES, LOUIS (1963), *Fiction for the Working Man*, Oxford University Press.

JOLLY, WILLIAM (ed.) (1879), *Education, its Principles and Prac-*

tice, as developed by George Combe, Macmillan.

JONES, R. ALUN (1938), 'Knowledge Chartism: a study of the influence of Chartism on nineteenth century educational development in Great Britain', Birmingham University M.A. thesis.

KAY-SHUTTLEWORTH, JAMES (1862), *Four Periods of Public Education as reviewed in 1832-1839-1846-1862*, Longman, Green.

KAY-SHUTTLEWORTH, JAMES (1846), *The School in its Relations to the State, the Church, and the Congregation*, Murray (edition of 1848; also reprinted in item above).

KELLY, THOMAS (1966), *Early Public Libraries. A history of public libraries before 1850*, Library Association.

KELLY, THOMAS (1957), *George Birkbeck: pioneer of adult education*, Liverpool, Liverpool University Press.

KELLY, THOMAS (1962), *A History of Adult Education in Great Britain*, Liverpool, Liverpool University Press.

KNIGHT, CHARLES (1864), *Passages of a Working Life during Half a Century*, Bradbury & Evans, 2 vols.

Lancashire Co-operator.

LEA, JOHN THOMAS (1968), *The History and Development of the Mechanics' Institutions*, Oldham, Research in Librarianship.

LEADER, ROBERT EADON (1897), *Life and Letters of John Arthur Roebuck*, Arnold.

LINTON, W. J. (1879), *James Watson: a memoir of the days of the fight for a free press in England and of the agitation for the People's Charter*, Manchester, privately published (edition of 1971).

London Scholastic Journal and Magazine of Education.

LOVETT, WILLIAM (1876), *Life and Struggles of William Lovett in his Pursuit of Bread, Knowledge and Freedom*, n.p. (edition of 1920, 2 vols).

LOVETT, WILLIAM (1853), *Social and Political Morality*, Simpkin, Marshall.

LOVETT, WILLIAM and COLLINS, JOHN (1840), *Chartism: a new organization of the people*, Watson (edition of 1969).

LOWE, R. A. (1972), 'Mutual Improvement in the Potteries', *North Staffordshire Journal of Field Studies*, vol. 12.

LUDLOW, J. M. and JONES, LLOYD (1867), *Progress of the Working Class 1832-1867*, Strahan.

LYTE, H. C. MAXWELL (1875), *A History of Eton College 1440-1875*, Macmillan.

MACCOBY, S. (1955), *English Radicalism 1786-1832: from Paine to Cobbett*, Allen & Unwin.

MCDONALD, JEAN (1965), *Rousseau and the French Revolution 1762-1791*, Athlone Press.

MACK, EDWARD C. (1938), *Public Schools and British Opinion 1780 to 1860*, Methuen.

MALTBY, S. E. (1918), *Manchester and the Movement for National Elementary Education 1800-1870*, Manchester, Manchester University Press.

MARCHAM, A. J. (1970), 'The "Myth" of Benthamism, the second Reform Act, and the Extension of Popular Education', *Journal of Educational Administration and History*, vol. ii, no. 2.

MARTINEAU, HARRIET (1849-50), *A History of the Thirty Years' Peace, 1816-1846*, n.p. (edition of 1858).

MARX, KARL and ENGELS, FREDERICK (1848, German edition), *Manifesto of the Communist Party* (English edition of 1946).

MATHEWS, H. F. (1949), *Methodism and the Education of the People, 1791-1851*, Epworth Press.

MEIKLEJOHN, J. M. D. (ed.) (1883), *Life and Letters of William Ballantyne Hodgson*, Edinburgh, Douglas.

MILL, JAMES (1818), 'Education', in *Supplement to The Encyclopaedia Britannica*.

MILL, JOHN STUART (1873), Autobiography, n.p. (edition of 1955).

MILL, JOHN STUART (1924), 'Speech on Secular Education', in *Autobiography*, (Oxford University Press edition, 1955, ed. Harold Laski).

MILL, JOHN STUART (1863), *Utilitarianism*, reprinted from *Fraser's Magazine* (edition of 1954).

MORGAN, WILLIAM (1815), *Memoirs of the Life of the Rev. Richard Price*, Hunter & Rees.

MORRIS, DAVID CARADOG (1952), 'The History of the Labour Movement in England, 1825-1852. The problem of leadership and the articulation of demands', London University Ph.D. thesis.

MUMFORD, ALFRED A. (1919), *The Manchester Grammar School 1515-1915*, Longmans, Green.

MUSSON, A. E. (1958), 'The Ideology of early Co-operation in Lancashire and Cheshire', *Transactions of the Lancashire and*

Cheshire Antiquarian Society, vol. 68.

NEW, CHESTER W. (1961), *The Life of Henry Brougham to 1830*, Oxford University Press.

OWEN, ROBERT, *The Book of the New Moral World*, Effingham Wilson, 1836.

OWEN, ROBERT (1820), 'Report to the County of Lanark', in *A New View of Society and other Writings* (edition of 1949).

OWEN, ROBERT (1858), *A Supplementary Appendix to the first Volume of the Life of Robert Owen ... 1803-1820*, vol. IA, Effingham Wilson.

PAINE, THOMAS (1791-2) *Rights of Man: being an answer to Mr. Burke's Attack on the French Revolution*, Johnson (edition of 1954).

PARKER, IRENE (1914), *Dissenting Academies in England*, Cambridge, Cambridge University Press.

PATTERSON, A. TEMPLE (1954), *Radical Leicester: a history of Leicester 1780-1850*, Leicester, University College.

The Plain Speaker. Edited by Thomas Cooper.

PLUMMER, ALFRED (1971), *Bronterre: a political biography of Bronterre O'Brien 1804-1864*, Allen & Unwin.

PODMORE, FRANK (1906), *Robert Owen*, Allen & Unwin (edition of 1923).

Politics for the People.

Poor Man's Guardian.

PRIESTLEY, JOSEPH (1791), 'A Discourse: the proper object of education in the present state of the world', in J. T. Rutt (ed.), *The Theological and Miscellaneous Works of Joseph Priestley*, vol. XXV, n.p., 1831.

READ, DONALD (1961), *Press and People 1790-1850: opinion in three English cities*, Arnold.

Report of the Proceedings at a Public Meeting in the Mechanics' Hall, Aberdeen ... 1851, on the important subject of national education (1851) Aberdeen, Lewis Smith.

ROBERTS, DAVID (1960), *Victorian Origins of the British Welfare State*, New Haven, Yale University Press.

ROBINSON, FREDERIC W. (1919), 'William Ellis and his Work for Education', London University M.A. thesis.

ROBSON, ADAM HENRY (1931), *The Education of Children engaged in Industry in England 1833-1876*, Kegan Paul, Trench.

ROSE, R. B. (1957), 'John Finch, 1784-1857; a Liverpool Disciple of Robert Owen', *Transactions, Historic Society of Lanca-shire and Cheshire*, vol. 104.

ROWE, D. J. (ed.) (1970), *London Radicalism 1830-1843*, London Record Society.

RUDÉ, GEORGE (1964), *The Crowd in History, 1730-1848: a study of popular disturbances in France and England 1730-1848*, New York, Wiley.

Rules for the Observance of the London Co-operative Society (1825), London Co-operative Society.

RUSSELL, BERTRAND (1934), *Freedom and Organization 1814-1914*, Allen & Unwin.

SALMON, DAVID (1905), *William Allen*, reprinted from *Educational Record*.

SALT, JOHN (1966), 'The Creation of the Sheffield Mechanics' Institute', *Vocational Aspect*, vol. xviii, no. 40.

SALT, JOHN (1971), 'Isaac Ironside 1808-1870: the motivation of a radical educationist', *British Journal of Educational Studies*, vol. xix, no. 2.

SAVILLE, JOHN (ed.) (1952), *Ernest Jones: Chartist*, Lawrence & Wishart.

SAVILLE, JOHN (1954), 'The Christian Socialists of 1848', in John Saville (ed.), *Democracy and the Labour Movement*, Lawrence & Wishart.

SCHOYEN, A. R. (1958), *The Chartist Challenge: a portrait of George Julian Harney*, Heinemann.

SEAMAN, W. A. L. (1954), 'British Democratic Societies in the Period of the French Revolution', London University Ph.D. thesis.

SEARSON, GEORGE R. (n.d.), *A Quarter of a Century's Liberalism in Leicester: what the Liberals did and how they did it, between the years 1826 and 1850*, Leicester, H. W. Batty.

Select Committee on the Education of the Lower Orders of the Metropolis (1816), HMSO (edition of 1968): evidence of Robert Owen.

SILVER, HAROLD (1965), *The Concept of Popular Education: a study of ideas and social movements in the early nineteenth century*, MacGibbon & Kee.

SILVER, HAROLD (ed.) (1969), *Robert Owen on Education*, Cambridge University Press.

SIMON, BRIAN (1972), *The Radical Tradition in Education in*

Britain, Lawrence & Wishart.

SIMON, BRIAN (1960), *Studies in the History of Education 1780-1870*, Lawrence & Wishart.

SLOSSON, PRESTON WILLIAM (1916), *The Decline of the Chartist Movement*, New York, Columbia College.

SMITH, EDWARD (1881), *The Story of the English Jacobins*, Cassell.

SMITH, F. B. (1973), *Radical Artisan: William James Linton 1812-97*, Manchester, Manchester University Press.

SMITH, SYDNEY (1957), 'Too much Latin and Greek', reprinted from *Edinburgh Review* in W. H. Auden (ed.), *Selected Writings of Sydney Smith*, Faber.

SOCIETY FOR THE DIFFUSION OF USEFUL KNOWLEDGE (SDUK) (1829), *Reports and Prospectus*, Baldwin & Cradock.

SPENCER, T. (1843), *Remarks on National Education*, Green.

STEWART, W. A. C. and MCCANN, W. P. (1967), *The Educational Innovators 1750-1880*, Macmillan.

Tait's Edinburgh Magazine.

Temple of Free Enquiry: a report of the proceedings consequent on laying the foundation stone of the Manchester Hall of Science, with an address by Robert Owen (1839), reprinted from the *New Moral World*, Leeds.

THALE, MARY (ed.) (1972), *The Autobiography of Francis Place (1771-1854)*, Cambridge University Press.

THOMPSON, DOROTHY (1971), *The Early Chartists*, Macmillan.

THOMPSON, E. P. (1963), *The Making of the English Working Class*, Gollancz.

TILLYARD, A. I. (1913), *A History of University Reform, from 1800 to the Present Time*, Heffer.

TYLECOTE, MABEL (1957), *The Mechanics' Institutes of Lancashire and Yorkshire before 1851*, Manchester, Manchester University Press.

UNION FOR PARLIAMENTARY REFORM ACCORDING TO THE CONSTITUTION (1812), *An Appeal to the Nation*, M'Creery.

VEITCH, GEORGE STEAD (1913), *The Genesis of Parliamentary Reform*, Constable.

WAKEFIELD, C. M. (1885), *Life of Thomas Attwood*, Harrison.

WALLAS, GRAHAM (1898), *The Life of Francis Place*, Longmans (edition of 1951).

WARD, J. T. (1970), *Popular Movements c. 1830-1850*, Macmillan.

WARD, W. R. (1965), *Victorian Oxford*, Cass.

WEARMOUTH, ROBERT F. (1937), *Methodism and the Working-Class Movements of England 1800-1850*, Epworth Press (edition of 1947).

WEARMOUTH, ROBERT F. (1948), *Some Working-Class Movements of the Nineteenth Century*, Epworth Press.

WEBB, R. K. (1955), *The British Working-Class Reader 1790-1848*, Allen & Unwin.

WEST, E. G. (1963-4), 'The Role of Education in Nineteenth-Century Doctrines of Political Economy', *British Journal of Educational Studies*, vol. xii.

WEST, JULIUS (1920), *A History of the Chartist Movement*, Constable.

Westminster Review.

WHITE, R. J. (1965), *Radicalism and its Results, 1760-1837*, Historical Association.

WICKWAR, WILLIAM H. (1928), *The Struggle for the Freedom of the Press 1819-1832*, Allen & Unwin.

WIENER, JOEL H. (1969), *The War of the Unstamped: the movement to repeal the British newspaper tax, 1830-1836*, New York, Cornell University Press.

WILLIAMS, DAVID (1955), *The Rebecca Riots: a study in agrarian discontent*, Cardiff, University of Wales Press.

WILLIAMS, GWYN A. (1965), *Rowland Detrosier: a working-class infidel 1800-34*, York, St Anthony's Press.

WILLIAMS, RAYMOND (1958), *Culture and Society 1780-1950*, Chatto & Windus (Penguin edition of 1961).

WILSON, ALEXANDER (1970), *The Chartist Movement in Scotland*, Manchester, Manchester University Press.

WILSON, BENJAMIN (1887), *The Struggles of an old Chartist*, Nicholson, Halifax.

WOODWARD, LLEWELLYN (1938), *The Age of Reform 1815-1870*, Oxford, Clarendon Press (edition of 1962).

WRIGHT, LESLIE C. (1953), *Scottish Chartism*, Edinburgh, Oliver & Boyd.

WYSE, THOMAS (1837), 'Education in the United Kingdom: its progress and prospects', Central Society of Education, *First Publication*, Taylor & Walton (edition of 1968).

YEAXLEE, BASIL A. (1925), *Spiritual Values in Adult Education*, Oxford University Press, 2 vols.